How to Take the Worry Out of Witnessing

George E. Worrell

BROADMAN PRESS
Nashville, Tennessee

To the youth who share Christ with their peers.
They shall be numbered in the Spiritual Hall of Fame.

Foreword

The youth generation is the greatest mission field in the world today! Young people are searching for the solution to life! Jesus Christ is that solution! That is why this book is so important.

Last year I asked several young people to meet with me for twelve weeks of training in discipleship and witnessing. We discussed things like: making Jesus Lord of your life; having a daily time alone with God; giving your money as God has given to you; memorizing Scripture verses. We were going great. Then I told them about the requirement to share their faith daily at school. What a blow! They looked like I had shot them! Would your reaction have been like theirs?

If so, this book is for you.

How to Take the Worry Out of Witnessing will help you to prepare spiritually for sharing your faith on a daily basis. Also, it will give you the practical, step-by-step "how to" of communicating the good news of Jesus Christ to another young person. You will discover that the author gives practical answers to some important questions. As you read the book, ask God to give you a deep and burning desire to share him with other people.

Allow me to say a word about the author. George Worrell and I have worked together in a ministry with high school students for several years. During that time we have built a deep friendship because of our common bond in Christ and because of our love for young people. As we have prayed together and worked together, I have seen George grow as a person in Christ. I have observed him as he has shared his faith—consistently and sensitively. I have worked with him in training others to share their faith. I saw his lifestyle very clearly one night when a girl shared how badly she was hurting in her life. George tenderly and lovingly, yet honestly, affirmed how God wanted to cleanse her and to use her. Because of what I have seen of the life of Christ in George Worrell, I have been challenged to develop my own witnessing lifestyle. I am confident that you will, as you read this book, catch George's spirit as he communicates to you the driving motivation of his life—to share Jesus Christ with people who need to know him.

One final word: You can read this book fifty thousand times and it will not make any sense until you get out there where people are—on your school campus or at work and begin boldly to share your faith in Jesus Christ!

"For I am not ashamed of the gospel: it is the power of God for salvation to every one who has faith" (Rom. 1:16, RSV).

BARRY ST. CLAIR

Preface

No matter how often one witnesses there seems to be a fragment of fear tucked away in the corner of the heart when it comes to sharing Christ with others. The causes of this fear are legion.

Satan is the author of fear. Such questions as: "Will my friends think I am a religious nut if I share Christ?"; "What if a person says no?"; "Should I share Christ now or wait until a better time?" are questions Satan causes us to ask. He will do his best to block our witnessing to friends. God has given Christians power over Satan. Second Timothy 1:7 says, "God hath not given us the spirit of fear; but of power, and of love, and of a sound mind." Perfect love casts out fear. Holy Spirit power is greater than Satan's power and his power makes for bold witnessing.

A coach of a recent Super Bowl team said, "Lack of experience can really hurt you in this game. Experience is still the number one guide to success in our business." [1] That is especially true with witnessing. Much fear comes from lack of experience. Think of the times when you have been nervous. Weren't you nervous when you sang your first solo before a crowd or played the piano at your first recital or taught your first Sunday School class during Youth Week at the church? A lack of experience always creates tension. The less you witness the more difficult it is. The more you witness the easier it becomes. Nothing will help to take the fear out of witnessing more than doing it. Someone has said, "Teaching is not necessarily telling. Learning is not necessarily listening. You learn to do by doing." Practice not only makes perfect—it takes fear away.

Another root of fear is ignorance. Lack of know-how causes us to shy away from witnessing. The book *How to Take the Worry*

[1] Tom Landry, *Star-Telegram* (Fort Worth), Tuesday, January 13, 1976.

Out of Witnessing is designed to help young people of all ages learn to share Christ in a simple, easy way. It is hoped that this manual will bring about a lifetime of sharing Christ.

To help youth leaders teach this book there is an appendix. In the appendix I have stated the purpose for each chapter, the materials needed for study, and have suggested creative procedures for teaching each chapter.

I would like to express appreciation to Barry St. Clair, Joe Ford, Rod Minor, Lamar Slay, Steve Cloud, Wayne and Michael McDill, Dr. Charles McLaughlin, and Dr. L. L. Morriss for their suggestions and encouragement. A special thanks goes also to my wife for her helpful insights and to the three young ladies who typed and retyped the manuscript. They are Jo Grey, Mary Lou Colquitt, and Melanie Gowan.

Contents

I

Is a Person Without Christ in Trouble?

A student worker attended a delightful winter retreat at Glorieta, New Mexico. His responsibility was that of teaching a heavy subject. It was the theology of evangelism. After several sessions the student worker got down to the nitty gritty. He said to the students, "You have the gospel. Why aren't you sharing it with your peers on campus?" There were several answers. One student said, "It's just not my thing." Another replied, "I don't know how." An athlete said, "I don't have time." After several minutes a young girl in the back raised her hand and made a startling statement. She said, "I just can't see that a person without Christ is in that much trouble."

Think about it for a moment. Which answer fits you? Perhaps the last reply hit the nail on the head. Many young people can't feel that it makes much difference whether a person accepts Christ or not. However, the Bible states the trouble of a Christless youth in a five-letter word. That word is

DEATH

Occasionally a young person will say, "Don't talk to us about death, judgment, and hell. Talk to us about life, living, and vitality." In reply I answer, "Thank you for your Pollyanna, rosy view of life. But remember that the Bible indicates that death is as much a part of life as living itself." Hebrews 9:27 states, "It is appointed unto men once to die, and then the judgment."

Hear this! The Bible states that there are three kinds of death. All are caused by sin. All represent a kind of separation.

9

Physical death—Are you familiar with the creation account in Genesis? Genesis 1-3 indicates that God created Adam and Eve. He put them in the Garden of Eden. He gave them the liberty to eat the fruit of all of the trees except one. That one tree was placed in the midst of the garden to test character and develop conscience in the lives of the first man and woman. Then Satan came along and said to Eve, "The Lord has said that you can't eat from any of the trees in the garden." She replied, "No, that's wrong. We can eat from all of the trees in the garden except one. If we eat of that tree we shall die." "No," said Satan, "you'll not die. God knows that fruit will make you become like him. You will have the ability to discern between right and wrong. Look at this fruit. It is good to eat and will make you wise. It is beautiful. Take and eat." Eve and Adam ate. They didn't die on that day, but they were separated from the garden in which grew the tree of Life. In time, they did die. Romans 5:12 says, "When Adam sinned, sin entered the entire human race. His sin spread death throughout all the world, so everything began to grow old and die, for all sinned" (TLB).[1] If you have been wondering why men die, you need wonder no more. We all die physically because we have all sinned. Lost young people need to know this.

Spiritual death—Ephesians 2:1 says, "You . . . who were dead in trespasses and sins." The moment a person sins,[2] he is immediately separated from God.

Let's suppose that on the day of your marriage, your husband moves to Paris, France and leaves you in your hometown. For twenty-five years you are separated. He knows you are alive. You know he is alive but he never writes, calls, telegraphs, and never sends greetings by friends. For all practical purposes, you would be dead to each other. So it is when you sin against God. At the

---

[1] *The Living Bible, Paraphrased* (Wheaton: Tyndale House Publishers, 1971).
[2] The content of sin will be discussed in a later chapter.

moment of wilful sin, you are separated from God. You are alienated from him. You are alive and he is alive, but for all practical purposes you are dead to each other. That is spiritual death.

Eternal death—Your friend who is spiritually dead and dies physically will be condemned to the eternal death. Revelation 21:8 says, "But the fearful, and unbelieving, and the abominable, and murderers, and whoremongers, and sorcerers, and idolaters, and all liars, shall have their part in the lake which burneth with fire and brimstone: which is the second death." The second death of this verse refers to an eternal separation from God. The worst thing about hell is that separation. All of this leads us to ask the question, "When your friends get where they're going, where will they be?"

God doesn't want your friends to experience eternal death. He wants them to have

LIFE

God wants each of his human creatures to have a happy, balanced, stable, useful life.

A Happy Life

Here is some good news. God wants his children to have a good time. We know that because he has given us a mind with which to create humor. He gave us a voice with which to chuckle, a mouth with which to laugh, and a funny bone. Furthermore, God's Son came to give us three cheers. Christ gives us the cheer of forgiveness, Matthew 9:2; the cheer of companionship, Matthew 14:27; and the cheer of victory, John 16:33. This victory includes victory over meaninglessness and death.

The cheers that Jesus gave are deep and inner. They swell during one's lifetime. They do not go away leaving hangovers and emptiness behind. That's the kind of happiness Jesus offers. It's the happiness you should share.

A Balanced Life

To God it is right for you to have a car, home, clothes, girl friends and boy friends. However, some people have everything and are still unsatisfied. Every achievement calls for another achievement and all leaves a vacuum in the heart. Jesus said, "Man shall not live by bread alone" (Matt. 4:4). What he was saying was that the most meaningful life is one that has a balance between the spiritual and the physical.

A Stable Life

Have you ever driven through a large city and noted the forest of television antennae attached to the houses and apartment buildings? These antennae give the television a good reception. In your wildest imagination picture a young person with television antennae on his head. The antennae are there so that the young person can sense the way the crowd is going and follow the vibrating wave lengths of the group. They are willing to follow every doctrine, taste every sin, experience the occult, and on and on. What is the result? A confused mind in a mad, mixed-up world. In contrast to this, God wants youth to have stability.

An illustration of the kind of stability God wants believers to have may be seen in the testimony given by Shirley Cothran, Miss America of 1975: "I was born into a Christian family which is one of the greatest privileges a person can have. My parents began taking me to the church nursery when I was three weeks old. I am thankful for their dedication. The church helped me to formulate the personality that I have now. It was in the church that I saw Christian adult examples, cultivated lasting friendships, and learned about Jesus.

"I was baptized when I was in the third grade. I accepted Christ intellectually but I did not have an experience with him. I came to grips with this fact and was actually saved several years later. When I became a Christian I received a stability in my life that helps me face my daily problems.

"Do I have problems? Yes, I have many and I can only make it as I face each new day with the help of the Lord. I can say that because of Christ I have never participated in drugs, alcohol, or sex. Various people have said, 'O come on, just this one drink.' But isn't it wonderful to say, 'No, no thank you.' Christ in me has given me the ability not to compromise on the things that are really important. That doesn't mean I never sin. I do, but God has given me a more stable life in Christ. I can truthfully say that I've never been sorry I became a Christian and I never will be. I only wish that all young people could know him as personal Savior." [3]

A Useful Life

There is an old adage that graces the wall of many a Christian home. It reads: "Only one life to live; 'twill soon be past. Only what's done for Christ will last." Jesus has many things he wants us to do for him. In fact, we were saved not only to go to heaven but to make our world a better place in which to live. Christ's purpose is that Christians make a contribution to science and the general welfare of man (Gen. 1:26), to our social structure (Mic. 6:8; Luke 4:18-19), and to the spiritual realm of life (Matt. 28:18-20). In the spiritual realm we are to be fishers of men (Mark 1:17). There is an excitement in fishing that is contagious. The sight of a huge swordfish straining against the line, jumping high into the air is majestic. A breathless battle between man and fish rages. At last the fish is landed. Man has a sense of satisfaction in knowing that he is the conqueror.

[3] This is an excerpt from a testimony given at the 1975 Texas Youth Evangelism Conference.

If that is exciting, think of the door to adventure Christ opened to Simon Peter, Andrew, James, John, and *you*. In fishing for people, mind is pitted against mind, heart reaches out to heart in love, and hands stretch forward to touch human need. The outcome is destiny. Can anyone compare the joy of soul fishing as against swordfishing?

That wraps it up—Christians serving under the Lord of the Universe to bring the real gusto of happiness, balance, stability, and usefulness to humanity. That is living. That's the kind of life God wants you to share with your lost friends.

Review

The person without Christ is in serious trouble. That trouble is death.

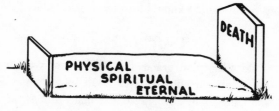

God wants all people to have life.

As a Christian you are responsible to inform your friends about the life God wants them to have

and

HOW THEY CAN HAVE IT!!!

11

What Does My Personal Life Have to Do with It?

Thomas was a fantastic basketball player. He made all-district and was popular among the students. He was a Christian who went to church on the one hand and to the keg parties on the other. After attending a church witnessing seminar, Thomas went to one of his buddies to talk with him about Christ. His buddy laughed at him and said, "You may be a Christian but I'm just about as good as you are. My answer to Christ is *NO*." Thomas was shocked but he learned the hard way that—witnessing is not only what you profess, it is how you live. There are several qualifications that you will need to be the best kind of witness. These include assurance, integrity and power.

Assurance Lends Authority

Confidence is necessary for success in any area. You young ladies would not go to a beautician who would say, "I am not sure I can fix your hair as you want it. It may not be the right color when I get through. It may be a little burned and shaggy, but if you will give me three hours of your time, I will try." Nor would a person fly with a pilot who lacks assurance in his ability to land an airplane once it is airborne. Just so, a lost person will not readily accept the witness of guys and gals who have doubts in their minds concerning their own salvation.

If you are going to introduce Christ to others, you must know that you know him. You can't introduce someone you don't know anymore than you can come back from some place you haven't been. A great man of the past has stated, "The zest and energy of the Christian life and its power to influence others depend upon the certainty with which salvation is realized." That's a long sentence. It simply means that the best witness is the one who is most sure of his salvation.

Christian Morality Points to Integrity

Psalm 51 was written after Nathan the prophet had confronted King David with God's judgment against him. It represents David's confession of sin. One of the most important insights on witnessing is found in verses 10-13. Here David prays, "CREATE IN ME A CLEAN HEART, O GOD; AND RENEW A RIGHT SPIRIT WITHIN ME. CAST ME NOT AWAY FROM THY PRESENCE; AND TAKE NOT THY HOLY SPIRIT FROM ME. RESTORE UNTO ME THE JOY OF THY SALVATION; AND UPHOLD ME WITH THY FREE SPIRIT. THEN WILL I TEACH TRANS-GRESSORS THY WAYS; AND SINNERS SHALL BE CONVERTED UNTO THEE."

This Scripture goes straight to the heart. The moral condition of your life has a great deal to do with your witness. The lost world will listen more readily if you try to measure up to Christian moral standards. Furthermore, God will bless your witness more readily if he can work through a vessel that is clean (v. 13).

Someone might ask, "Do I have to wait until I'm perfect before I can witness?" If you wait that long, you'll never do any witnessing. In your approach to the lost, admit that you have faults and failures. Show how Christ helps you to be better than you would be without his uplifting presence in you.

On the other hand, don't try to get away with murder. You may think sin is private but it is public. You can't be a witness if you are sexually involved with your girl friend or cheating on tests or always telling dirty jokes and going to every keg party you get a chance. If that's your story, people won't listen to you and God won't honor your witness. James 4:4 is true. "Evil pleasures of this world—make you an enemy of God" (TLB).

Many times people say that "living the life" is being a witness. Others say that "speaking verbally about Jesus" is being a witness. There seems to be a contradiction. David's life was not "living the life" *or* "being a verbal witness," but it was "living the life *and* being a verbal witness." They go together. You cannot separate them. If you have one without the other, your witness is incomplete.

Just as an airplane has two wings, so your witness has two parts: the life you live and the words you speak. If you are flying at thirty thousand feet and the pilot says, "One of our wings must be dropped," which one do you want to drop—the left one or the right? It would be a disaster to drop either one of them. As long as you are flying, neither should be dropped. This is true of our witness. Both living the life and sharing Christ verbally are mandatory. We cannot drop either one without "crashing" in our sharing life.

A word should be said about being a Jesus freak—don't be one. Being a "holier than thou" person is as deadly to witnessing as being a hypocrite. You can live your holy life without condemning others. For instance, if someone invites you to go out for a beer you might answer, "No, thanks, but I will have a Coke with you sometime." Or, if you are asked to go somewhere you had rather not go, you can respond, "Thanks! I am not interested in that but let me know when you are going to a concert, (game, club meeting, etc.) and I will go with you." [1] By suggesting an alternative, the person realizes you are not rejecting him. The door to future witnessing is still open.

Time Alone with God Empowers

Fruitful soul-winners all testify that a time alone with God is a must for effective witnessing. A public testimony about Christ is impossible without private tutoring from Christ.

[1] Paul E. Little, *How to Give Away Your Faith* (Downers Grove, Illinois: Intervarsity Press, 1966), p. 42.

In the daily quiet time you have fellowship with God through Bible study. The Bible is the Christian's toolbox. Out of the Bible comes intelligent ways of meeting excuses and animosities. Just as the physician does not prescribe the same medicine for each case, so the same Scripture will not cause the truth to break in on every person. It is for this reason that the teenager needs to be familiar with the Word of God. Another reason is that the Word is the sword of the Spirit which God uses to bring conviction. There is power in God's Word that is absent in human comment.

Do I hear some teenager say, "Look, I'm not an adult. I can't be expected to study the Bible and know it at my age." Why not? When Paul wrote to young Timothy, he complimented him for studying the Word from an early age. Second Timothy 3:15 says, "You know how, when you were a small child, you were taught the holy Scriptures; and it is these that make you wise to accept God's salvation by trusting in Christ Jesus" (TLB). Don't sell yourselves short.

Steve Davis was the starting quarterback for three years at Oklahoma University. During those years his team lost only one game. He was known as a guy who had a football in one hand and the Bible in the other. Steve not only read the Bible daily, he memorized hundreds of verses of Scripture. He said, "When I read the Bible, I read a passage, then I pray it back to God. I meditate on it and try to apply it to my life. Scripture memorization helps me when sharing my faith." If Steve can do it, you can, too. Why don't you pattern your Bible reading after his?

1. Read your Bible every day.

2. Set a definite time, preferably in the morning. Of course, don't limit your Bible study to set periods. Refer to it throughout the day.

3. Pray before reading and ask God to open your eyes to what he wants to say to you.

4. Pray the verses back to God.

5. Look for specific things. "Most people don't find anything special in the Scriptures because they are not looking for anything in particular." [2]

6. Read through the Bible once a year.

7. Memorize God's Word. Set your goal to memorize at least two verses a week.

Another important factor of daily quiet time is prayer. In Bible study God speaks to you. In prayer you speak to God. Don't pray only when you feel like it, or you will never pray. Prayer is a matter of practice and you learn to pray best by praying.

Barry St. Clair has suggested that we ought to have a daily quiet time because God desires our fellowship. That is a staggering thought. When God and I get together God gets joy, satisfaction and pleasure from being with me. That is almost too much for me to understand. I can't grasp it.

That pretty much shoots down our usual ideas that we read our Bibles and say our prayers so that we will be good boys and girls. That is so petty when we learn that God wants to meet us morning by morning and day by day.[3]

In your daily quiet time, you will want to pray for the lost. There is more to praying for the lost than just saying, "God, save the lost." Our prayers should be specific. Ask yourself, "For whom am I praying by name every day?" A helpful instrument to keep your mind on the names of the lost is a prayer list. Jot the names of a lost friend on the fly leaves of your Bible. Place the date by the names and leave a space for God's answer. One person prayed for thirteen years before his friend was saved. Stick to praying for others and never give up.

[2] Leroy Eims, *Winning Ways* (Wheaton, Illinois: Victor Books, 1974), p. 131.

[3] Barry St. Clair, *Time Alone With God* (Oklahoma City: Arthur Davenport Association, 1975).

In praying for the lost, pray that the Holy Spirit will open and enlighten their eyes. Since the lost person is blinded by Satan (2 Cor. 4:4), you should pray that Satan's power over the lost would be broken. Next pray for God to send Christians to witness to the lost person (Acts 8:26). Finally, pray that the lost will bend their wills to Jesus Christ until Christ is received as Lord and Savior.

The other day a young person said, "I don't need to pray for the lost so much as I need to pray for myself that I will have the courage to witness." Well spoken! The reason you don't talk to young people about God is because you are not talking to God about young people.

Pray that God will burden your heart for your lost friends until you are constantly aware of their utter depedence on you. Pray that he will help you to develop finesse and tact in witnessing. Pray everyday until God moves you to share Christ.

III

Introducing God's Hidden Persuader

The work of salvation is the work of God. It is God who moves the unconverted to the place where Christ is accepted as Lord and Savior. God does his moving work through his Hidden Persuader, the Holy Spirit. The diagram that follows quickly pictures the work of the Hidden Persuader.

The Holy Spirit Convinces

The Holy Spirit convinces the unconverted of the historical truth about Christ. Second Corinthians 4:4 states that the god of this world (Satan) "hath blinded the minds of them which believe not, lest the light of the glorious gospel of Christ, who is the image of God, should shine unto them." This verse indicates that the lost have been blindfolded. They cannot see the truth about Christ. The Holy Spirit takes the blindfold off so that the non-Christian can see that Jesus was the historical Son of God. By the power of the Holy Spirit a person recognizes that Jesus was pre-existent (Col. 1:16-17), came in the flesh (John 1:14), lived a perfect life (Heb. 4:15), died on the cross for our sins (1 Pet. 1:18-19), was raised from the dead (Luke 24:5-6), is coming again (Acts 1:11), and will accept all who know him (Matt. 10:30-33).

No one can become a Christian without believing these basic facts about Jesus. No one will believe these facts without the convincing work of the Holy Spirit. The Holy Spirit does not do his revealing work as a mysterious magician who pulls rabbits out of a hat. Rather, he uses preaching, the Bible and witnessing.

This is the point of Romans 10:13-15: "Anyone who calls upon the name of the Lord will be saved. But how shall they ask him to save them unless they believe in him? And how can they believe in him if they have never heard about him? And how can they hear about him unless someone tells them? And how will anyone go and tell them unless someone sends him? That is what the Scriptures are talking about when they say, 'How beautiful are the feet of those who preach the Gospel of peace with God and bring glad tiding of good things'" (TLB). In other words, how welcome are those who come preaching God's good news!

Has it ever dawned on you? The Holy Spirit will reveal truth through you as you witness to your friends!

The Holy Spirit Convicts

John 16:7-11 describes the Holy Spirit's ministry as a convictor. THE HOLY SPIRIT CONVICTS MEN OF THE NATURE OF SIN. At the heart of human experience is an unresolved problem of evil which has filled the pages of history with tragedy. This evil has brought our modern world to the brink of chaos. It is not that men today are any more evil than those of the past. It is simply that modern technology has placed in their hands greater powers of destruction than any age has ever known. What is the nature of this dimension of the demonic which poses so great a threat to our world? What is the nature of sin?

Able men have given serious thought to this problem and have reached a variety of conclusions. To Socrates, sin meant ignorance. To Aquinas, sin meant rejection of church dogma. To Augustine, sin meant being away from God. To Stalin, sin meant disobedience to the state. To some young people today, sin means identification with the establishment. There are other conclusions which men have reached regarding the nature of men. It is the task of the Holy Spirit to change the thinking of men about sin and to help them see it for what it really is. The Holy Spirit seeks to convict men that sin is basically rebelling against God. It is the rejection of God's revelation of himself at every level. Most of all, sin is the rejection of God's supreme revelation in Jesus Christ. Jesus said, "And when he comes, he will convince the world of sin and of righteousness and of judgment: of sin, because they do not believe in me" (John 16:8-9, TLB).

THE HOLY SPIRIT CONVICTS MEN OF THE WAY IN WHICH THEY MAY BECOME RIGHTLY RELATED TO GOD. Once again, various men have given various ways to be reconciled to God. There are those who have imagined that a right relationship with God could be inherited. Still others have supposed that sincerity guarantees a right relationship with God. Some believe that good works open the door to fellowship with God. It is the task of the Holy Spirit to change the thinking of men and help them to comprehend the right way to come to God. The Holy Spirit convicts men that a right relationship with God is possible only through faith in the crucified and risen Christ.

Finally, THE HOLY SPIRIT CONVICTS MEN REGARDING THE VERDICT OF THE CROSS. Jesus said, "And when he comes, he will convince the world of . . . judgment" (v. 8, TLB). In Christ's day the sinister powers of evil were arraying themselves to contend against God. The action moved swiftly to a spectacular climax. When the last echo of the enemy's reviling had been absorbed, Jesus was found nailed to a cross. A conflict had been waged. A verdict had been reached. A judgment had been rendered. What was it? What happened on a hill called Golgotha.

Once again men have been divided in their opinion of the cross. Some have found in Christ's cross an offense to the mind. Read 1 Corinthians 1:18. Others have dismissed the cross as just one more execution of an idealist.

The Holy Spirit helps men rethink the meaning of the cross. He helps them know that the cross represents God's judgment upon the prince and evil ruler of this world. The cross represents the decisive struggle between God and the powers of evil. The resurrection which followed proclaimed the mighty triumph of Jesus over sin and death. This judgment did not remove evil from the face of the earth. However, the death of Jesus broke the dominion of death, destroyed the power of Satan, and assured God's ultimate triumph over evil.

In summary, unless a man is convicted that he is lost in sin and needs to be saved and that Christ is the way to God, he will never be converted. It is the Holy Spirit who does this convicting.

The Holy Spirit Draws

In John 6:44 Jesus said, "No man can come to me, except the Father which hath sent me draw him." The way the Father draws men to Jesus is by the Holy Spirit.

One day my daughter came in from school and said, "I'm so hungry I could eat a horse and a bear." She meant it. Have you ever been that hungry? It is the Holy Spirit who makes lost persons intensely hungry and thirsty for Christ. He makes them want to want Christ so much that they will say yes to him.

Right now in your high school or junior high, there are many young people with whom the Holy Spirit has already worked. They are seeking souls. They are ready to say yes to Christ.

The Holy Spirit Changes

When a person says yes to Christ, a change is made in the heart. "Therefore if any man be in Christ, he is a new creature: old things are passed away; behold, all things are become new" (2 Cor. 5:17). Becoming a new creature is an experience which Christ dubbed a rebirth. Rebirth is a mysterious, definite, instantaneous, lasting change that comes by the Holy Spirit. Jesus said in John 3:5, "Except a man be born of water and of the Spirit, he cannot enter into the kingdom of God." The Holy Spirit cleanses and renews (Tit. 3:5). The Holy Spirit transforms.

Most of us remember the fairy tale of Pinocchio. It is the story of how a wooden puppet became animated by the touch of the fairy's wand. The promise was made that if the wooden puppet would tell the truth and do a good deed he might become a real live boy. The conclusion of the story was that Pinocchio became a live boy with conscience, soul and spirit.

That transformation was spectacular, wasn't it? But there is a transformation that is even more incredible. Upon acceptance of Christ, the Holy Spirit transforms a person from God's enemy to his adopted child. That's breathtaking!

The Holy Spirit Indwells

The Holy Spirit enters the heart of the lost at the moment of conversion. First Corinthians 6:19 says that the body of the Christian becomes the actual temple of the Holy Spirit. Think about the process of becoming a Christian—from an unacceptable, unclean vessel to a unique home for the Spirit of Christ.

Put into plain, everyday language the Bible tells us that the burden of proof in witnessing lies on the Holy Spirit's shoulders and not on ours. HE IS THE HIDDEN PERSUADER.

IV

So Where Do I Come In?

Since salvation is the work of God, Christians can relax and let him do the work. But wait a minute! God needs Christian young people through whom he can work, so—here are some principles that relate to you, the Holy Spirit, and witnessing.

Be Available

Jesus said, "As my Father hath sent me, even so send I you" (John 20:21). Christ has sent us to witness for him, but we must be willing witnesses. We must be available to let him do his work through us. You probably thought that God needed your abilities. You thought that God needed your intellectual achievements, your spiritual knowledge, your logic, your ability to debate the gospel. All God really needs is for you to be a willing witness, just to be available. *God doesn't need your ability; he needs your availability.* A black boy puts it this way, "I don't try to figure God out. I just try to be ready when God wants me."

You will be interested in knowing that some encouraging things are happening in our world today. Awakenings are breaking out in various countries. In the Philippines a 16-year-old boy came out of the mountains to the village market. He asked a missionary for a Bible. The missionary was so busy he almost disregarded the request. Something compelled him to hunt up a Bible and give it to the boy. Four months later a group of the mountain people asked for a missionary to come to their town. Forty-six people had responded to the gospel. It was a 16-year-old boy that took them the good news. God can use you in that way if you will be available.

Hang Loose

There is a motto that will change your entire attitude toward witnessing. It is: "SUCCESSFUL WITNESSING IS SHARING CHRIST IN THE POWER OF THE HOLY SPIRIT AND LEAVING THE RESULTS TO GOD." [1] This motto will take away the fear of failure. For instance, on one occasion I was traveling to Houston by plane. I sat next to a young lady who was reading a book called *The Exorcist.* I said to her, "Do you believe in demons?" "Yes." "Do you believe in the devil." "Yes." "I assume you believe in God." "Yes, I do." In the course of the conversation, I asked if I might share the plan of salvation. She readily agreed. At the end of the interview I asked her if she would accept Christ as personal Savior. She said no. I gave my testimony and again asked her to make a commitment. The second time she refused. I asked her if she had problems with which we might deal. She shared several. I tried my best to help. I gave her an opportunity to trust Christ once more, but she refused. When we got out of the airplane and started down the long marble hall of the Houston airport, I was concerned about a young lady who had rejected Christ. However, I was not defeated. I had shared Christ in the power of the Holy Spirit and had left the results to God.

On that same day I visited with a University of Houston pre-law student. He was looking for a house to rent. In the course of conversation, I said, "You're looking for a home on earth. I wonder about your home in heaven." He said, "I'm not sure about that." I replied, "Would you let me take a minute to read you this pamphlet entitled 'How to Have a Full and Meaningful Life?' " He said, "Sure." We read through the pamphlet, came to the prayer, and he received Christ into his heart.

On another occasion Kathy Christy, a high school student from Pasadena, and her friend Priscilla were distributing New Testaments from their church. As they visited the different houses it seemed like no one had time to talk, especially about Jesus. Then they met

---

[1] Gil Stricklin and George E. Worrell, *Lay Evangelism School in the Local Church* (Baptist General Convention of Texas, Evangelism Division), pp. 138-139.

Kirk. He was fifteen and searching. They soon found that he didn't know much about Jesus and he knew nothing at all about how to become a Christian. It was a perfect time to tell him how Christ died on the cross to save everyone, and how God desired to have a deep, growing, personal relationship with him. He said he had never understood that before. When they asked him if he would like to ask Jesus to come into his life, he hesitated. Priscilla shared how she came to Jesus and about the purpose her life now had. Then Kirk said that he really did want to know Christ. He was afraid to pray by himself, so the girls led him in a prayer in which he asked Jesus to forgive him of his sins and to dwell in his life. The two girls went away rejoicing.

In the last two instances, the persons said yes to Christ. However, these two witnessing experiences were no more successful than when the first person said no. Perhaps you would object. After all, the second two people said yes to Christ. That's true. However, in all three cases Christ was shared and the results were left to God.

You must leave the results to God. Anchor this fact firmly to your fear problem. In doing so "you will find yourself facing up to the mainstream of a Christian's responsibility and opportunity rather than drifting downstream into the jagged rocks of discouragement and embarrassment." [2]

The Lord doesn't ask you and me to work for him. He asks us to let him do his work through us. One thing is certain. The more you witness, the greater number of people God will bring into his Kingdom through you.

Be Sensitive

Sensitivity to the leading of the Holy Spirit will prevent the witness from becoming an extremist—being pushy on one hand or never witnessing at all on the other. Young people must be sensitive to

[2] Ken Anderson, *A Coward's Guide to Witnessing* (Carol Stream, Illinois: Creation House, 1972), p. 64.

the Holy Spirit within them if they are to know when to approach a person, what subject to start with, how far to go, when to press for a decision, and when to allow time for thinking. One person puts it, "For every piece of ripe fruit there must be a willing worker. Don't bruise the fruit." Experience, failures, rebuffs, encouragements help to make us aware of the Spirit's leadership. To have know-how in witnessing, a person must witness. So make a start and keep it up.

Be Filled

Today's wavelengths are full of letters signifying various things. Almost everyone knows what STP, LSD, ESP, and PTL mean. Here's a new one for you—HSP. It means Holy Spirit Power. That power comes as we are completely controlled by Christ and his Spirit. Being filled with the Holy Spirit is so important to witnessing that the next chapter will deal entirely with this experience.

V

The Power Keys

On the day of Pentecost the Holy Spirit came initially upon the church. The immediate result of his coming was that the disciples spoke "the mighty works of God" (Acts 2:11, RSV). The ultimate result was that three thousand people were converted in one day (Acts 2:41). In Acts 4:8, the effect of the fullness of the Holy Spirit in Peter was boldness to proclaim the gospel. Acts 4:21 points to the results, "All men praised God for what had happened" (RSV). Acts 6:1-7 indicates that Spirit-filled men were chosen to minister to the needs of the early church. As a result, the word of God spread, the number of disciples multiplied greatly in Jerusalem, and a great many priests were obedient to the faith (v. 7). When Saul was converted, he, too, was filled with the Holy Spirit (Acts 9:17). Immediately, he began to proclaim Jesus in the power of the Holy Spirit.

Obviously, the success of verbal witnessing is dependent upon inner spiritual resources. It wasn't enough that the disciples had been with Jesus for three years. It wasn't enough that they had heard his masterful teaching, viewed his miracles and experienced his resurrection. They had to be empowered by the Holy Spirit.

Have you ever experienced HOLY SPIRIT POWER? It is one thing to know about the power for witnessing; it is another to claim that power. Furthermore, it is one thing to say be filled with the Holy Spirit and another thing to say how. The following steps will give you necessary keys to the Spirit-filled life.

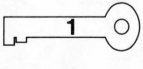

The first step is to recognize that the Holy Spirit lives within you permanently because of the new birth (1 Cor. 6:19).

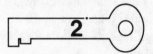

Realize that it is God's expressed will that you be filled (completely controlled) by his Spirit. This fullness is his provision for saving your life and making it full and meaningful (John 10:10b).

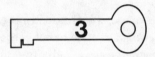

Next, you must thirst. Meditate on John 7:37-39. Verse 39 suggests that the living water is the Holy Spirit. The only time you gladly and willingly take a drink of water is when you are thirsty. You will not receive the fullness of the Holy Spirit unless you desire or thirst for this fullness. Answer these questions: Are you satisfied with your life as it is? Do you really want Christ to control your thoughts, deeds, words? If so, do you want the Holy Spirit to set your "self" aside and enthrone Jesus in your heart so that he will no longer occupy a secondary place? You must abandon yourself to God and his will (Gal. 2:20).

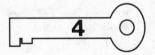

If you are thirsty, then you can move on to the requirement of dealing with sin. In Ephesians 4:30 Paul says, "Do not grieve the Holy Spirit of God, in whom you were sealed for the day of redemption" (RSV). Read Ephesians 4:25-31. Underline the various sins listed in this passage. In these verses Paul listed lying, nursing a grudge, theft, bad language, meanness, bad temper, quarreling, harsh words and dislike of others as sins which especially grieve the Holy Spirit. These sins and many others hinder the Spirit's total control of one's life. Young people must face their sins honestly.

Are you ever conscious of:

A secret spirit of pride: an exalted feeling, in view of your success or position; because of your good training or appearance; because of your natural gifts and abilities, an important, independent spirit?

Love of human praise: a secret fondness to be noticed; love of supremacy, drawing attention to self in conversation; a swelling out of self when you have had a free time in speaking or praying?

The stirrings of anger or impatience, which, worst of all, you call nervousness or holy indignation; a touchy, sensitive spirit; a disposition to resent and retaliate when disapproved of or contradicted; a desire to throw sharp, heated flings at another?

Self-will: a stubborn, unteachable spirit; an arguing, talkative spirit; harsh, sarcastic expressions; an unyielding, headstrong disposition; a driving, commanding spirit; a disposition to criticize and pick flaws when set aside and unnoticed; a peevish, fretful spirit; a disposition that loves to be coaxed and humored?

Carnal fear: a man-fearing spirit; a shrinking from reproach and duty; reasoning around your cross; a shrinking from doing your whole duty by those of wealth or position; a fearfulness that someone will offend and drive some prominent person away; a compromising spirit?

A jealous disposition, a secret spirit of envy shut up in your heart; an unpleasant sensation in view of the great prosperity and success of another; a disposition to speak of the faults and failings, rather than the gifts and virtues of those more talented and appreciated than yourself?

A dishonest, deceitful disposition; the evading and covering of the truth; the covering up of your real faults; leaving a better impression of yourself than is strictly true; false humility; exaggeration; straining the truth?

Unbelief; a spirit of discouragement in times of pressure and opposition; lack of quietness and confidence in God; lack of faith and trust in God; a disposition to worry and complain in the midst of pain, poverty, or at the dispensations of Divine Providence; an overanxious feeling whether everything will come out all right?

Formality and deadness; lack of concern for lost souls; dryness and indifference; lack of power with God?

Selfishness; love of ease; love of money? [1]

By prayer, hold your heart open to the searchlight of God. "Search me, O God, and know my heart: try me, and know my thoughts: and see if there be any wicked way in me" (Ps. 139:23,24).

First John 1:9 indicates that God has made provision for restoring fellowship by means of our confession. To confess means to agree with God on those things which hinder the fullness of the Holy Spirit in our lives. To be filled we must acknowledge our sins and repent of them. When confession and repentance are complete, a giant spiritual step is made toward being filled by the Spirit.

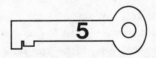

Finally, one must trust. Read John 7:37-38 again. Notice that Jesus said, "If any one thirst, let him come to me and drink. He who believes in me, as the scripture has said, 'Out of his heart shall flow rivers of living water' " (RSV). The words "he who believes in me"

indicate that to be controlled by the Spirit, a person must trust Christ completely.

F. B. Meyer was a young man who realized that he could not do God's work in his own power. He confessed sin, yielded his will and prayed. Something blocked the filling of the Spirit. At last as he walked down a lonely road, he prayed, "Lord, I've done everything I know and failed. What more must I do to receive your Holy Spirit?" It seemed as though he heard God's voice, "F. B., just as by faith you received salvation from the hands of the crucified Christ, so by faith you must receive the infilling of the Holy Spirit from the hands of the resurrected Lord."

At this, Meyer said, "Lord, just as I breathe in this warm air tonight, so by faith I receive your Holy Spirit to control my life."

What happened? F. B. Meyer did not see a bright light. He did not have an ecstatic experience or speak in tongues. The Person of the Holy Spirit flooded his life, giving him power to witness to God's Son, Jesus Christ.

That brings us again to the definition of successful witnessing: SUCCESSFUL WITNESSING IS SHARING CHRIST IN THE POWER OF THE HOLY SPIRIT AND LEAVING THE RESULTS TO GOD.

God is eager for you to experience the Spirit-filled life. If you are ready to begin a new spiritual pilgrimage, please pray the following prayer:

> Dear Lord: I confess my sins and ask you to take complete control of my life. I am willing to die to self. Thank you for giving me salvation by faith. By the same faith I claim the fullness of your Holy Spirit. Be my daily companion and Lord. Accomplish your will, and love the world through me. I pray this in the name of the Father, the Son, and the Holy Spirit. Amen.

Sooner or later you will know that the Holy Spirit is quietly filling your life. Keep on believing; the filling will be yours day by day.[2]

[1] Author Unknown, "Not I, But Christ."
[2] George E. Worrell, "How to Have the Spirit-Filled Life" (Baptist General Convention of Texas, Evangelism Division), p. 15.

VI

Witnessing Is Not That Hard

The very fact that you are reading this book and perhaps attending a school of evangelism indicates something really great! YOU ARE INTERESTED IN SHARING CHRIST. Your interest, however, doesn't mean that you have no hang-ups about witnessing. Perhaps you feel that witnessing is just too hard. It takes too much knowledge—too much time—too much courage—too much everything. Hold it right there. You are trying to make witnessing too difficult.

God uses our efforts no matter how feeble they are. Edward Kimball was D. L. Moody's Sunday School teacher. Moody was a non-Christian and Kimball decided it was time to witness to him. Accordingly, he made his way to the shoe store where Moody was working. Before he arrived he began to wonder whether this was the right time. If the other clerks saw him talking with Moody, they would ask him who Kimball was; then they would tease Moody about being a goody-goody boy, and the whole matter would be muffed.

Under the pressure of this conflict Kimball passed the shoe store once and was about to give up the project. The Holy Spirit gave him courage and he dashed into the store and asked to see Dwight L. Moody. Moody was in the back of the store wrapping shoes. Kimball went into the back room and the following drama unfolded:

> I went up to him at once, and putting my hand on his shoulder, I made what I afterwards felt as a very weak plea for Christ. I don't know just what words I used, nor could Mr. Moody tell. I simply told him of Christ's love for him and the love Christ wanted in return. That was all there was. It seemed the young man was just ready for the light that then broke upon him, and there, in the back of that store in Boston, he gave

himself and his life to Christ.[1]

Dwight L. Moody became America's greatest evangelist.

You have already learned that successful witnessing is sharing Christ in the power of the Holy Spirit and leaving the result to God. Let me add the other side of that coin.

WITNESSING IS CARRYING ON A RELAXED CONVERSATION BETWEEN TWO PEOPLE ABOUT CHRIST.

In conversation with others what do you do? You talk and you listen. Often, conversations will be carried on for years as you relate to the person from day to day.

Talking

You can't tell a person about Jesus without talking. Talk about things that are of interest to you and to your lost friend. One problem you want to overcome is monopolizing the conversation. Conversation about Christ should be a two-way street between you and the other person.

Relaxed Conversation

Confident of the Lord's guidance and free from the sense of pressure or embarrassment, you ought to be natural as you introduce spiritual themes. In your witnessing you ought to be as relaxed in your tone of voice and demeanor as you are when you are discussing last night's game or your physics assignment. Don't ever try to force the issue. To do so will do more harm than good. Actually you will discover so many people who are interested in spiritual reality that you won't have to force yourself on those who are not interested. It will be an enormous relief to you when you discover that you

[1] Mendell Taylor, *Exploring Evangelism* (Kansas City: Beacon Hill Press, 1964), p. 501.

can legitimately drop the subject if, after trying to begin a conversation about Christ, you do not discover a response prompted by the Holy Spirit.[2]

A friend of mine witnessed to a Krishna follower in the Atlanta, Georgia airport. Everything he sought to say about the true Jesus was blocked. He tried and tried but no response. My friend did not feel intimidated. He didn't go away like a cowed dog who crawls to his master on his stomach. No, he went away with a deep satisfaction that he was faithful in sharing Christ AND THAT IS ALL GOD ASKS.

Listening

Make no mistake about it. Listening is as important or perhaps even more so than talking.

Listening helps non-Christians realize that you feel they are important. If you dominate the conversation, they will get the feeling that you are trying to get something over without considering their feelings. Most people would give anything to find someone who will listen to them. When you listen long enough, you will begin to know and understand the individual. You will also gain his gratitude and in the process find a willingness to listen to the story of Christ you want to tell.[3]

Listening helps one to discover the needs of others. Everyone has needs. One of the best ways to lead your friends to Christ is to find their need and use it to present Christ as the answer. One witnessing book calls this procedure "scratching people where they itch." [4]

Boredom with life, deep meaninglessness, guilt, aching loneliness, insecurity, and a thousand other things bug young people. Christ

[2] Little, *op. cit.*, page 36.

[3] *Ibid.*, page 32.

[4] Ralph W. Neighbour and Cal Thomas, *Target Group Evangelism* (Nashville: Broadman Press, 1975), p. 20.

has the answer to these problems, and you can communicate these answers.

Suppose your friend loses a parent by divorce. This experience often crushes young people. They feel lonely—sometimes unwanted—resentful—frustrated. One day your friend gives you an opening to meet her need. You can say that Christ would be a constant companion. His love for us is deeper than that of our parents. Christ will guide so that she won't make similar mistakes in marriage. He will comfort her in the lonely hours.

Suppose that you know a teenage alcoholic. He gives you an opportunity to help. You can point to Ephesians 5:18: "Be not drunk with wine, wherein is excess; but be filled with the Spirit." You can tactfully suggest that all attempts of escapism and ecstasy through alcoholism are but cheap substitutes for the real thing. Jesus can give a high that is lasting and deep—one that doesn't need to be rekindled daily or hourly.

A promiscuous girl might share her frustration with you. You can explain that no sexual experience can completely satisfy the needs of any individual. Sex without God leaves a person incomplete.

Many are laughing on the outside and crying on the inside. Here's the place to begin. Meet their need, be a friend, sympathize and build them up.

Continuous Conversation

Conversations can last for months and even years. Teenagers may say yes to Christ upon the first hearing. This is often the exception and not the rule. Sometimes you must cultivate a person over a period of time. The cultivation process is illustrated with Nicodemus. His first encounter with Christ was in John 3. Obviously, Nicodemus had heard Christ speak or had heard others speak about him to the degree that he sought him out. In the first encounter, Jesus told Nicodemus how it is, but pressed no decision on him. It was one of those "think-about-it" encounters. The next reference to Nico-demus comes some two years later when he defended Jesus in a private session with his fellow Pharisees (John 7:50,51). Clearly, Nicodemus was not yet a follower; he had only moved from "seeker" to "sympathizer." The next reference to Nicodemus is much later, nearly a year, when he joined Joseph in claiming the body of Jesus for burial (John 19:39, 40). That was a three-year period of cultivation.

This kind of evangelism recognizes that much witnessing is seed-sowing rather than harvesting, and that many witnesses may share in the cultivation process.[5] However, you must be careful that you don't forget to reap. If all you do is cultivate the crop and never harvest, the crop will be lost.

In Alabama, Sam took John to Sunday School and church with him occasionally. He gave him a pamphlet about Jesus and asked him to read it. Sam never got around to talking with John to ask him to trust Christ. It was his back trouble that kept him from it. He had a yellow streak running down his back. One night John had a serious motorcycle accident. He almost died. Sam prayed for John. He promised God that he would share Christ with his friend at his first opportunity. When John was moved out of the intensive care ward, Sam witnessed to him. John readily trusted Christ but he said one thing that burned into Sam's mind: "Sam, I thought you would never ask me to trust Christ. You almost waited too long." In his own words Sam says, "Now, I try to get to the point of my witnessing earlier. I don't want someone else to miss Christ by my negligence."

Well, there you are. The truth that witnessing is a relaxed conver-sation between two people about Christ ought to take some of the sweat out of your witnessing, but remember witnessing is *urgent*. Someone is waiting on a good word about Jesus from you *now*.

[5] David Haney and Elton Trueblood, "You Are a Witness," *Target: Lifestyle Evangelism and Lifestyle Ministry* (Memphis: Brotherhood Commission).

VII

The Best Thing You've Got Going for You

"May I tell you the greatest thing that has ever happened to me? As far back as I can remember, I have believed in freedom to do what I wanted to do. I didn't hurt anybody and certainly believed in God. I had this friend in high school. He wasn't a 'Holy Joe,' but a really great guy. One day he began telling me about having Jesus Christ living inside him. I thought he was a nut! But it bothered me, so I began to go to church with him. Gradually I began to realize that I had stolen my life away from God, and sooner or later I would have to give it back to him. Well, I was nearly eighteen when I finally turned my life over to Jesus Christ. I didn't see any visions, but ever since I have felt his life in me. The great thing is not so much that I accepted him, but that he accepted me. Sometimes I think it's like being plugged into an electric socket! Know what I mean? Has this happened to you, too?" [1]

This testimony parrots the many testimonies recorded in the New Testament. "Come, see a man who told me all that I ever did," urged the woman of Samaria (John 4:29, RSV). "Though I was blind, now I see" was the straightforward testimony of the blind man (John 9:25, RSV). "We have found the Messiah," cried Andrew to Peter (John 1:41, RSV). Paul declared, "I was on such a mission to Damascus, armed with the authority and commission of the chief priests, when one day about noon, sir, a light from heaven brighter than the sun shone down on me and my companions. We all fell down, and I heard a voice speaking to me in Hebrew, 'Saul, Saul, why are you persecuting me? You are only hurting yourself.' 'Who are

---

[1] Ralph W. Neighbour, "Witness, Take the Stand!" (Baptist General Convention of Texas, Evangelism Division), p. 34.

43

you, sir?' I asked. And the Lord replied, 'I am Jesus, the one you are persecuting. Now stand up! For I have appeared to you to appoint you as my servant and my witness. You are to tell the world about this experience and about the many other occasions when I shall appear to you' " (Acts 26:12-16, TLB).

These experiences point to the fact that the best thing you've got going for you is your testimony. One's personal testimony is a powerful weapon. Imagine what would happen if all Christians on your school campus began sharing their personal testimony with others.

Value of the Testimony

The value of the personal testimony is limitless. Think of it for a minute. A personal testimony catches attention and holds the interest of the non-Christian. It establishes empathy and is very difficult to refute. A prominent senator once said that when he speaks to students on campus, he tells them that he has had a dynamic experience with Christ. No one can dispute his personal experience.

The Director of Evangelism for the Navigators tells of a college student in Idaho who said, "You Christians live in a dream world. What you're saying about a new life is too good to be true." A girl heard this comment and said, "No, it's not a dream. It happened to me last year." Then she gave her testimony. The guy listened and was silenced by the authenticity of the student's personal experiences. Your testimony is the best answer for skeptics. It is not theory or philosophy but factual history. At a point in time in a real world, you live it.[2]

Think Your Testimony Through

All Christian young people should be able to share their Christian testimonies with others. The best way to have confidence in giving

[2] Eims, *op. cit.*, p. 100.

one's testimony is to prepare the testimony beforehand. In thinking through and writing your own testimony, study Paul's experience recorded in Acts 26:1-29.

Paul began his testimony by describing his life before he became a Christian (Acts 26:4-12). He was born in Tarsus and schooled in Judaism (v. 4). He was a strict Pharisee who conscientiously interpreted and obeyed the Jewish laws and customs (v. 5). As a good Pharisee, he believed in the resurrection of the dead.

When Paul came into contact with people who claimed to have truth superseding orthodox Judaism, he was naturally horrified. His first reaction was that of hatred. His hatred led him to oppose the Christian movement violently (v. 10).

The next part of Paul's testimony described how God began to deal with his rebellion. God intercepted Paul on his journey of Christian persecution. A miraculous light far beyond the brilliance of the sun suddenly overwhelmed Paul and his companions. Jesus, the risen Christ, spoke in no uncertain terms: "Saul, Saul, why do you persecute me? It hurts you to kick against the goads" (Acts 26:14, RSV).

God does not have one particular way to confront individuals. In Paul's case, Jesus had to use drastic means to confront an unbeliever. This same Jesus called Matthew while he was at work and spoke to Zacchaeus on the streets of Jericho. The miracle is not in *how* Jesus speaks, but *that* he speaks to unworthy people at all. A person can never be the same after he meets God. For Paul, this was the beginning of a new way of life. His experience with Christ was so important that it became the underlying theme of all he wrote and preached. He knew that Christ had transformed his life and that Christ would transform anyone who accepted him.

Read Acts 26:19-29 again. These verses indicate that Paul was not disobedient to his vision from heaven. He gave his testimony beginning in Damascus, going throughout Jerusalem, Judea, and to all parts of the world. For every time Paul's conversion experience with Christ is recorded in Scripture, he must have shared his testimony hundreds of times.

In studying the experience of Paul you have noted that his testimony fell into three or four categories. As you begin writing your own testimony, you may wish to use the following outline:

1. What my life was before I became a Christian.
2. What caused me to want Christ as my Savior.
3. How I became a Christian.
4. What being a Christian means to me.

Rules for the Game

Consider these suggestions as you prepare your testimony. Keep it short. Paul's testimony is most compact. It omits every side issue and all points that are immaterial to the main subject. If your testimony is too long, a lost person may not allow you to finish it.

Tell the truth. Not everyone has a testimony that brings him from marijuana to the Master, or from prison to the pulpit. Unlike Paul, most people will never see a bright light when Jesus confronts them. Be sure you avoid the temptation to embellish your story for dramatic effect. Be honest in appraising your Christian experience. Be genuine with yourself. In this way, the truth of your experience will come through to others.

Make Christ central. Paul referred to Jesus and his work over and over in his testimony. In developing your testimony, be careful not to focus too sharply on yourself and your personal feelings. Major on what Christ has done for you and what Christ can do for them.

Stay away from "church" words. For example, the word *Christian* may mean "being moral" to some, "church member" to many, and "non-Jew" to others. How many ways do you think the word *sin* can be defined? Words like *saved, convicted, born again, lost, regen-*

eration, and *repent* may mean nothing to the unbeliever. Consider the following example given by Ralph Neighbour: "I stood in the church, afraid to go forward. I was convicted and wanted to get saved. Finally, I stepped into the aisle and was washed in the blood of the Lamb." The unbelieving student to whom such a testimony is given might be mentally reacting in the following way: "Why did he have to go forward? In my church we do that only to receive Holy Communion. I thought 'conviction' was something that happens to criminals in courtrooms. 'Saved'—isn't that a word holy rollers use? What on earth was a dead lamb doing in the aisle?" Can you understand why the unbeliever quickly changed the subject?

Keep your testimony up-to-date. Share what Christ did for you this morning and what his relationship is with you now.

Be enthusiastic. Paul's testimony was so enthusiastic that he had the attention of King Agrippa, Festus, and all the others of the court. One way to be enthusiastic in your testimony is to relive it as you tell it.

Look over the following testimonies. How do you think they stack up with the rules given above?

"I was reared in a home where my mother was a gracious Christian. My father professed to be a Christian, but his actions indicated that he was everything but what a Christian ought to be. There was so much difference between my mother and my father in action, words, deeds and attitude that I knew that I didn't want anything that would make my dad act like he acted. I wanted whatever there was about my mother that made her act like she acted. The difference between the two was God."

As a young boy I attended a religious meeting. One of my best friends said to me, "Sonny boy, wouldn't you like to commit your life to Christ and invite him to be your Lord and Savior?" I said, "Yes." That day I heard God say to me, "I want you." And I said, "All right, God, I give myself to you—everything I am and everything

I will be." I was so young I didn't know what I was getting into. Everything I got into was good. I've been disappointed in people, circumstances and situations, but I've never been disappointed in Jesus Christ. Christ helped me to get an education through high school and college. He has given me a beautiful purpose in life. Have you ever had an experience with Christ?"

John Cather of Florida testifies: "About a year and a half ago, while I was working in construction, I felt a real need in my life for something better than I had. My job was paying well, and I had a lot of friends, but something inside of me was never at rest. I began to read a small Bible that had been given to me while I was at the University of Florida.

"Last January I was playing basketball in a league, and an old friend of mine happened to be on the other team. After the game he came up to me and asked me what was I up to as far as my life was concerned. I told him I had been reading a lot of books about personal relationships and also the Bible. I discovered that he was a Christian and was involved in 'Reach Out' ministries. He invited me to their Wednesday night 'Joy Explosion,' and even though I didn't know what that was, I accepted his invitation.

"By the next Wednesday I had decided to be open-minded to all that was going on, and after a few songs and prayer together, an appeal was given to accept Christ personally. The words bore right into me in a way that I'd never felt before. I knew I needed Christ in my life but I was still not strong enough to turn to someone and let them help me.

"As the other young people were leaving, my friend and several others talked with me in the prayer room and I came to the realization that there wasn't any sense in waiting until a later time to accept Christ. As I repeated a prayer after my friend, fantastic joy filled my heart. It is the best moment of my life.

"Since then I've been involved in Bible study and disciple groups that have helped me grow tremendously. I am now 21 and I pray I'll be faithful until he calls me home. Wouldn't you like to know Christ, too?"

Write out your testimony several times and polish it. Practice it with Christians until it becomes natural. Then pray for opportunities to share it with your lost friends. Sharing your testimony is seed-sowing. It will change your life—AND THEIRS.

Preparing Your Testimony

1. How my life was before I became a Christian:

_____

_____

_____

_____

_____

2. What caused me to want Christ as my Savior:

_____

_____

_____

_____

_____

3. How I became a Christian:

_____

_____

_____

_____

_____

4. What being a Christian means to me:

_____

_____

_____

_____

_____

VIII

How Do I Get Started?

You have learned to give your testimony. You will learn the plan of salvation by heart. You are now ready to share. You envision talking with a lost person. A haunting question rings in your mind. "What do I do first? How do I get started?"

It is simple. Take a deep breath and relax. Say to yourself, "Witnessing is nothing but a relaxed conversation between two people about Christ." Whenever you relax you'll make the lost person feel at ease. Secondly, introduce yourself and begin to talk. Guide the conversation by asking questions. In the conversation you will want to build a bridge of communication. That bridge will help to move the lost person from secular thinking to thoughts about the spiritual.

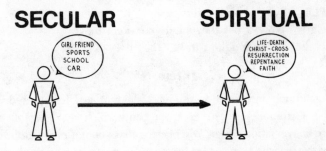

Walk the person from the secular to the spiritual step by step. Don't try to jump the span in one broad jump.

In your conversation, talk about general things, move to more personal things, then narrow the conversation to spiritual things. The following acrostic will help move the conversation smoothly as you talk with a stranger.

F — family or friends
I — interests
R — religion (use neutral words)
M — message

Family or Friends

Before talking about supernatural things, you will want to talk about natural things. By doing this you will win the person's friendship and confidence. If you dive right into a religious conversation the lost person may say to himself, "Boy, that's a religious *nut*." When you talk about the things in which the lost person is interested, he will say, "Boy, he's a regular guy. I like him." So the first thing you do is ask general questions and talk about family or friends.

Chris: Phil, where does your dad work?
Phil: He works at the hospital as an X-ray technician.
Chris: Do you have brothers and sisters?
Phil: I've got four sisters.
Chris: Wow, I bet they spoil you, don't they?
Phil: I hate to admit it, but they do.

Interests

Be genuinely interested in the interests of others. Jesus is and you can be. Common interests create a bond which makes frank and sincere conversation easier. Discovering that you both play golf, that you both are radio hams or are interested in poetry can be an opening wedge. Size the person up. If you see a motorboat in the garage, you can assume that the young person likes water skiing or fishing. Bowling trophies give a clue to bowling interests. If you see a football in the room, talk about sports.

Chris: Phil, are you on the football team?
Phil: I play halfback.

Chris: You look like you are fast. Are you on the first string?

Phil: Yeah, I guess I'm lucky.

Religious Background

In moving to a discussion of the religious background, use neutral words. Neutral words are words that do not arouse opposition to the subject of Christianity. The neutral words in the following conversation are Roger Staubach and the church.

Chris: Phil, did you know that Roger Staubach of the Dallas Cowboys is a fantastic Christian?

Phil: Well, I heard something about that.

Chris: Do you and your folks go to church anywhere?

Phil: We used to go before Dad started working on Sundays.

Note that Phil was not asked if he were a Christian. This question is deceptive because some think that they are Christians if they are not atheists. Nor was the question, "Have you ever been saved?" asked. The word *saved* is a dangerous tension-creator. The less tension you create, the better.

Chris: Phil, tell me. Have you ever made the wonderful discovery of knowing Jesus personally, or are you still in the process? [1]

Phil: I guess I'm still in the process.

Hooray! You have crossed the bridge and you are still communicating. Notice three things about the above question. It refers to knowing Christ in a personal way (John 17:3). It refers to a wonderful discovery. Finally, the person with whom you are talking does not have to say no in the conversation. The question put words in Phil's mouth.

After the response by Phil, move to your personal testimony by

[1] Additional questions that could be asked:
Do you ever think much about spiritual things?
If someone were to ask you what is a real Christian, what would you tell him?

saying, "Phil, I know where you are. I was once there myself." Then give your testimony.

A Longtime Friend

The above approach may be altered for use with a longtime friend. The following conversation will show you how to make an approach with someone you have been cultivating.

> Chris: Hey, Phil, I have something I've been wanting to talk to you about. Could we get together for a Coke sometime?
>
> Phil: A Coke sounds good to me. When do you want to go?
>
> Chris: How about right now?
>
> Phil: Sure.

Go to a drive-in. While drinking your Coke in the car, direct the conversation as follows:

> Chris: Phil, I want to ask you to forgive me for something.
>
> Phil: Really? What's that?
>
> Chris: We've been friends for a long time. We've had lots of fun together and our relationship means a lot to me, but I've never talked to you about your relationship with Christ. I'm going to admit to you that I'm not perfect. There are a lot of things in my life of which I'm not proud, but in spite of my ups and downs, I would like to share with you what Christ means to me. (Give testimony here and proceed with witnessing interview.)

Now, my young Christian friends, that's how you begin. Some of you with sharp minds will notice that we have left out the word *message* in our acrostic "FIRM." We have talked about friends, interests, and religion. We moved into the witnessing interview, but we didn't get to the message. You're asking, "Where is the message?" Cheer up, that's the topic for the next chapter.

IX

A Witnessing Tool

How many pamphlets have you seen that tell a person how to meet Jesus? One youth worker has collected as many as twenty-seven. Ecclesiastes 12:12 might rightly be paraphrased, "Of the making of many pamphlets there is no end."

Many people feel that pamphlets such as "Real Life," "How to Have a Full and Meaningful Life," and "A Master Plan for Your Life" make witnessing easier. The reasons are obvious. Witnessing booklets are tools. Every craft has its tools whether it is a surgeon's scalpel, a lawyer's case books or a carpenter's hammer. A witnessing brochure is a tool which can be used with success because it is easy to carry, simple but all-inclusive. It contains the plan of salvation, Scripture verses, a built-in invitation and follow-up material. Each young person would do well to master a pamphlet that enables him to share Christ easily with others.

Introducing the Pamphlet

There are several methods by which a pamphlet can be introduced. They are as follows:

1. "It has always been hard for me to share Christ in a way that makes sense. I have discovered this little booklet which really helps. May I share it with you?"

2. "I have been reading a booklet and I would like for you to give me your opinion of it."

3. "Have you ever seen a booklet that tells a person how to be a Christian? I have one and I would like to share it with you."

4. God will give you other ways to introduce the booklet. Let him lead you.

Sharing the Pamphlet

As you share the pamphlet, be sensitive to the person through the Holy Spirit's leadership. There are some simple rules to follow when sharing the booklet.

1. Read the booklet as it is. On one occasion I was visiting with a college student from the University of Houston. It took him thirty minutes to read through a booklet to a lost man. Normally, it takes only nine minutes to read it. That is a no-no. Don't try to explain the content of the Scripture verses in the booklet. Let the Holy Spirit do the convincing and the convicting.

2. Hold the booklet so that it can be clearly seen by the person to whom you are reading it.

3. Defer questions that arise until the end of the pamphlet. If, as you are reading the pamphlet, someone asks you a question, say, "That's a good question. Would you mind if we wait until we finish reading the booklet before we answer the question?" The reasons for doing this are obvious. In the first place, the question may be answered as you proceed through the booklet. In the second place, the person to whom you are reading may be trying to get you sidetracked so that you won't ever get to the prayer of invitation. In the third place, you may not know how to answer the questions. If that's true, be honest and suggest that you will try to find out and pay the person a return visit.

4. Use a pencil to point to the paragraph you are reading. This will help the person focus his attention on what you are saying.

5. If a person appears disinterested, ask the question, "Does that make sense to you?"

6. If you make a boo-boo while reading the pamphlet, just keep reading. How many of you have ever played in a piano recital? If you make a mistake and keep playing, no one will know of your mistake except your mother and the piano teacher. If you

stop and start over, everyone will know. An eighth-grader from Calvary Church in Lubbock, Texas, shared Christ with a twenty-one-year-old man. She was so nervous that he had to help her pronounce some of the words. When he came to the prayer time, he committed his life to Christ.

7. If someone has already heard of the pamphlet, ask the person what he thought of the booklet. If he has any questions about it and is interested in the gospel go over the booklet again.

One great Christian leader has suggested that when we get to heaven we will probably find millions of people there because of witnessing pamphlets. One such person is Bert Tucker from Georgia. Bert was discharged from the Army. He went to New Orleans for a big time before taking a job. He was getting out of his car at the motel when two fellows walked across the street. "Excuse us," they said. "Are you a Christian?" He told them where to go. They handed him a pamphlet. He wadded it up before their eyes and put it in his pocket. When he got in that night and emptied his pockets, he put the pamphlet on the desk. He woke up the next day with a hangover. The pamphlet had not moved.

"I picked up that pamphlet and found myself on my knees reading. I found my Lord right then and there. I shall eternally be grateful for the two boys who gave me that pamphlet."

Spoken words vanish in the air. Printed words never fade. This truth should encourage the strong use of pamphlets. Carry several booklets with you at all times. Give them away by the dozens. Leave the results to God.

X

You Can Develop Your Own Plan

Suppose you master a pamphlet and become dependent upon it. Suppose the Holy Spirit impresses you to speak to someone about Christ. You feel in every pocket or look through all the clutter in your purse and there is no pamphlet. You're frustrated. You can't share Christ without the booklet, so you walk helplessly away. What a tragedy! Every young person should memorize God's plan of salvation so well that he could share the plan at any time and under any circumstances.

Furthermore, don't you think that there is some value in being able to take the New Testament and share God's plan of salvation with others? Some persons feel that there is an added authority in using the Bible—perhaps so. One student uses John 3:16 and shows the cause of salvation (God's love); the cost of salvation (God gave his only begotten Son); the condition of salvation (whosoever believeth); and the result of salvation (everlasting life). Others like to use the book of Romans to share the basic plan of salvation.

I would suggest that you memorize the following plan. It is one which has been taken from various witnessing booklets and personalized. This means that over the years I have made the plan my own. The plan will take the form of a conversation between Chris and Phil.

The Plan

Chris: Just as the world is ruled by physical laws, there are spiritual laws that lead to the ultimate reality of God. The first principle is: *God loves you.* Isn't it wonderful that God loves you?

Phil: Yes, it is.

Chris: God wants you to have two things. First, he wants you to have *an abundant life on earth*. In John 10:10b Jesus said, "I am come that you may have life and have it more abundantly." What does the word *abundant* mean to you?

Phil: It means full.

Chris: That's right. It means full, overflowing, happy and satisfying. That's the kind of life God wants you to have on earth. He also wants you to have *an eternal life in heaven*. John 3:16 says, "For God so loved the world that he gave his only begotton Son that whosoever believeth in him should not perish but have everlasting life." Isn't it wonderful that God wants us to have an abundant life on earth and an eternal life in heaven with him?

Phil: You can say that again.

Chris: The second truth is this: *Man has separated himself from God by sin.* Phil, what does the word *sin* mean to you?

Phil: I guess it means to do something wrong.

Chris: That's correct. Sin is when you know that something is wrong and you go ahead and do it anyway. It means when you know that something is right but you don't do it. James 4:17 says, "Remember, too, that knowing what is right to do and then not doing it is sin." Sin is missing the mark. It is rebelling against or living independently of God. You can sin in your thoughts as well as your actions. The Bible says in Romans 3:23 that all have sinned. Phil, does the word *all* include you? Have you ever known that something was wrong and you just went ahead and did it anyway?

Phil: I'm human, aren't I?

Chris: Phil, Romans 6:23 says that the wages of sin is death. Death means separation. If I were to have a heart attack and fall over dead, I couldn't talk to you and you couldn't talk to me. Right?

Phil: Right.

Chris: Then, when we have sinned against God, we have been separated from him. Here is a picture that shows our separation.

<u>God — Holy</u>

Separation

<u>   </u>

Man — Sinful

Once we have been separated from God, we can't get back to him through keeping the Commandments, church membership, good works, religion or philosophy.

If we die separated from God on earth, we will always be separated from God in the world to come. Jesus calls that separation hell. Phil, God does not want you to be separated from him and here is some good news.

God has made a way for us to come back to him through Jesus Christ. Here is another picture.

[1] Irving Childress, "The Big Plus" (Arizona State Convention, Evangelism Division).

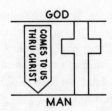

Now let's think about Jesus! Who was Jesus?

Phil: He was God's Son.

Chris: Did Jesus ever sin?

Phil: No.

Chris: That's correct. He was perfect. What did Jesus do that we might be saved?

Phil: He died on the cross.

Chris: If Christ were perfect, he did not die on the cross in punishment of his own sins. Rather, he died on the cross in punishment for our sins. Having died for our sins that we might be rightly related to God, Jesus said in John 14:6, "I am the way, the truth, and the life: no man cometh unto the Father, but by Me."

Note the way we get to God:

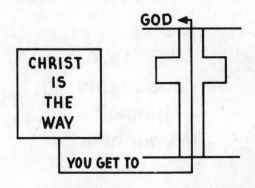

Phil, do you see the way the line goes through the cross to God?

   Phil: Yeah.

   Chris: There is something else you need to know:

You must receive Jesus Christ as your personal Savior in two ways:

   1. You must receive Christ by faith. Ephesians 2:8-9 says, "For by grace are ye saved through faith; and that not of yourselves: it is the gift of God: Not of works, lest any man should boast."

   2. Furthermore, you must receive Christ by invitation. Jesus said in Revelation 3:20, "Behold, I stand at the door [of your heart], and knock: if any man hear my voice and open the door, I will come in to him, and will sup with him, and he with me."

   Here are two pictures:

Phil, which picture represents your life? Is Christ on the outside of your life, or is he on the inside of your life?

   Phil: Well, I guess he's on the outside of my life.

   Chris: O.K. The very moment you say, "I am sorry for my sin and I now invite Christ into my heart to save me from my sins," Christ will come in.

Then the picture looks like this: Christ X's out your sin

and plants himself in your heart.

Phil, Christ then takes up his home in your heart.

Phil, would you be willing to invite Jesus Christ into your heart?

Phil: Yes, I would.

Chris: All right, let's pray and invite Christ to be your Savior. Repeat this prayer after me: Dear Lord, I know I have done wrong and need forgiveness.

Phil: Dear Lord, I know I have done wrong and need forgiveness.

Chris: Thank you for dying for my sins and for offering me eternal life.

Phil: Thank you for dying for my sins and for offering me eternal life.

Chris: Please forgive my sins and help me to turn from them.

Phil: Please forgive my sins and help me to turn from them.

Chris: I now confess you as my Lord and receive you as my Savior.

Phil: I now confess you as my Lord and receive you as my Savior.

Chris: Take control of my life and help me to become all you want me to be. In Jesus' name. Amen.

Phil: Take control of my life and help me to become all you want me to be. In Jesus' name. Amen.

Chris: Did you accept Christ as your Lord and Savior?

Phil: Yes, I did.

Chris: Where is Christ now?

Phil: He is in my heart.

Chris: How do you know?

Phil: Because he promised.

Chris: Phil, there's another Scripture I would like to call your attention to. It's found in Romans 10:13. It says, "Whosoever shall call upon the name of the Lord shall be saved." Did you call upon the name of the Lord?

Phil: Yes.

Chris: Then from this day on and this hour, you can know that you are a Christian.

There is one other subject I would like to cover before leaving. Have you ever run a footrace?

Phil: Sure.

Chris: When you say, "On your mark, get set, go," is that the beginning or the end of the race?

Phil: That is the beginning.

Chris: That's right, Phil, and when you accepted Christ it was not the end of the Christian race, it was only the beginning. Do you know what the goal of the Christian life is?

Phil: Not exactly.

Chris: The goal of the Christian life is to become like Jesus. Romans 8:28 and 29 says, "And we know that all things work together for good to them that love God, to them who are the called according to his purpose. For whom he did foreknow, he also did predestinate to be conformed to the image of his Son, that he might be the firstborn among many brethren." The way we become more like Jesus can be seen in the following diagram:

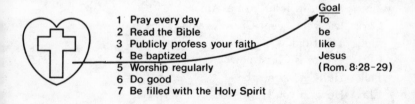

1 Pray every day
2 Read the Bible
3 Publicly profess your faith
4 Be baptized
5 Worship regularly
6 Do good
7 Be filled with the Holy Spirit

Goal
To
be
like
Jesus
(Rom. 8:28-29)

The more like Christ you become on earth, the greater your reward will be in heaven. Do you have any questions about what you have done?

Phil: I'm sure I will as I go along, but right now I'm really happy.

Chris: Could we pray together before I leave?

Phil: Sure, let's do.

Chris: Dear God, thank you for saving Phil. We pray that you will help him to grow in Christ that he might become one of the best Christians who has ever lived upon the face of the earth. In Jesus' name, Amen.

Phil, tell your friends what has happened in your life. This will mean a lot to you and to them. Let's get together tomorrow for a Coke.

Phil: O.K. Thanks, Chris, for talking with me. No one ever told me about these things before. I'll see you later.

Conclusion

The way to learn this plan of salvation is for you to get your pencil right now and start writing it. Rewrite it as many times as is necessary for you to learn it. Practice sharing the plan with a Christian buddy. Ask for help to find the weaknesses in your thinking and communication. The more you share, the less clumsy you will become.

XI

What Do I Do
When My Friend Says Yes?

Suppose you were married. In a few years you had a baby. After the birth of the baby, the doctor said: "Congratulations! Your baby is born. He is healthy and normal. Now the work is done. That's all there is to it." Wouldn't you protest? Wouldn't you say, "Wait a minute. The work is not done. It has only begun."

In like manner, every Christian witness should understand that evangelism without follow-up is totally incomplete. Introducing a friend to Jesus and then turning your back on him as you pursue other lost people is like bringing a baby into the world and telling him to fend for himself.

Genuine evangelism demands as much time and effort after the student makes his profession of faith as it did before conversion. The goals of every Christian witness should be two. First, introduce others to Christ. Second, stay with the new converts until they have been integrated into the church, built up spiritually, and taught to win others to the Lord Jesus Christ. Nurturing new Christians has been called spiritual pediatrics. It is the parental care given new converts to bring them into spiritual maturity and fruitfulness.

Paul considered himself a parent to those he introduced to Christ. To the Corinthians he wrote, "For though you have countless guides in Christ, you do not have many fathers. For I became your father in Christ Jesus through the gospel" (1 Cor. 4:15, RSV). Paul called Titus and Timothy his sons in the faith. Following the example of Paul, the Christian witness should adopt each new convert as his own spiritual son or daughter. Say to yourself, "I will do everything I can to help my spiritual children grow up in Christ."

Think of the needs of the new convert. Every baby needs love.

Jesus said, "This is my commandment, that you love one another as I have loved you" (John 15:12). Christlike love is to be the foundation of all attempts to give parental care to spiritual babies. If you genuinely love those to whom you witness, you will give them time. You will be patient with their childish ways. You will be gentle with them.

Another need is nourishment. As babies must have food, so must babes in Christ receive nourishment. To Simon Peter, Jesus said, "Feed my lambs . . . Feed my sheep" (John 21:15,17). Note that Jesus said "Feed my lambs" before he said "Feed my sheep." Lambs will not become sheep unless they are fed. Children will not become mature adults until they have nourishing food. The divine formula for infant feeding is the milk of the Word. First Peter 2:2 says, "Like newborn babes, long for the pure spiritual milk, that by it you may grow up to salvation" (RSV).

At first it will be a matter of your feeding the new converts. In time new believers should come to the place where they are able to feed themselves. Finally, they will come to the point where they will want to and be able to feed others. The goal for all Christians is "the measure of the stature of the fulness of Christ" (Eph. 4:13).

Spiritual babies need more than nourishment, they need protection. First Peter 5:8 says, "Be sober, be watchful. Your adversary the devil prowls around like a roaring lion, seeking some one to devour" (RSV). What prey would be more alluring than new believers? Major areas of temptation in which Satan attempts to ensnare new converts are sex, security, and success: "the lust of the flesh, and the lust of the eyes, and the pride of life" (1 John 2:16).

In addition to help in fighting temptation, new Christians need protection against false doctrine. In Ephesians 4:14-15, Paul says, "So that we may no longer be children, tossed to and fro and carried about with every wind of doctrine, by the cunning of men, by their craftiness in deceitful wiles. Rather, speaking the truth in love, we are to grow up in every way into him who is the head, into Christ" (RSV). The antidote to believers being carried away from the truth by deceivers is simple: "Be no more children."

Parental care also involves training. Proverbs 22:6a says, "Train up a child in the way he should go." The moment you introduce others to Jesus Christ, you ought to begin training them in witnessing, Bible study, prayer, obedience and a daily walk with the Lord. Paul said in 2 Timothy 2:2, "What you have heard from me before many witnesses entrust to faithful men who will be able to teach others also" (RSV). Don't allow the new converts to think that witnessing is for the preacher or for the professional. Part of the joy of being a Christian is introducing Christ to others. Take the new convert with you the next time you witness.

The Bible gives three distinct procedures for nurturing new Christians in the faith.

Personal Contact

Personal contact was a method both Jesus and Paul used to help Christians grow. Jesus chose twelve men "to be with him" (Mark 3:14, RSV). These disciples were "his regular companions" (TLB). Considering Jesus' example, the personal contact procedures of follow-up evangelism might be called the "with him" principle.

The same method was employed by the apostle Paul (see 1 Thess. 3:10-11; Acts 15:15-36). Acts 14:21-22 says, "When they had preached the gospel to that city and had made many disciples, they returned to Lystra and to Iconium and to Antioch, strengthening the souls of the disciples, exhorting them to continue in the faith." The words "strengthening the souls of the disciples" are a striking testimony to the importance of personal contact. Paul was even willing to risk his life to exhort the new Christians to continue in the faith.

Just as Christ and Paul found it necessary to spend time with their disciples, so you must project your life into the lives of converts. Casual, social contact during church functions is not enough to make a strong impact. This is a part of the cost of being a witness. While it may take from twenty minutes to two hours to help the lost say yes, it may take from twenty weeks to two years to help the new Christian get on his feet spiritually. Neglected children often become delinquent. Neglected converts also become delinquent. To avoid spiritual delinquency, you must give yourself to the new babe in Christ.

Personal Prayer

Personal prayer was vital for Paul, and his letters record his frequent and fervent praying for those who were Christians. To the Philippians Paul said, "Praying earnestly night and day that we may see you face to face and supply what is lacking in your faith" (1 Thess. 3:10, RSV). He wrote to the Romans, "For God is my witness, whom I serve with my spirit in the gospel of his Son, that without ceasing I mention you always in my prayers" (1:9, RSV).

The prayers of Paul are good models for our own intercession for new converts. You may wish to keep a diary of all of those whom you introduce to Christ. Record the date, the time, and the nature of the conversion experience. Keep a record of the progress of the new convert's growth. Pray for that person through the years.

Personal Correspondence

Personal correspondence is the third follow-up method employed in the New Testament. When a personal visit by an aposotle was an impossibility, a letter was sent instead. Over half of the books of the New Testament are letters written to encourage believers in the faith.

At times, conflicts will keep you from making a personal visit with the new convert. Write a letter to show your concern. Your letters should encourage the application of Bible truths to life because God promises to bless us through his Word. Bible studies as enclosures in follow-up letters can be helpful.

All of these procedures—contact, prayer, correspondence—will tell the new converts that you are definitely interested in their personal lives. The worth of such interest is indescribable.

The following steps summarize the ministry to each new convert:

1. Share the new convert's name with your pastor and Sunday School director.

2. Bring the person to church with you.

3. Encourage a public profession and baptism (Matt. 28:18-20).

4. Introduce the person to your friends. Include him in your daily activities.

5. When possible, become a prayer partner with the new convert.

6. Help the person begin a daily Bible study program.

7. Keep in touch by telephone.

8. Pray for the new convert.

Witnessing to the lost and seeing them say yes to Jesus is a great joy. An even greater blessing is to see those whom you have led to Christ grow in the Lord and win others. That's follow-up.

XII

How to Deal with Hang-ups

On Thursday night Betsy had made a public profession of faith in Christ and had asked for believer's baptism. On Friday morning the pastor went to her dad's shop to invite him to the baptismal service. They talked about the daughter's decision. It was discovered that the father was not a Christian. Before the pastor could say anything, the dad said, "Preacher, I'd like to be a Christian more than anything I know, but I can't. My business takes all my time."

Mr. Jones's excuse is just one of many given for not following Christ and not identifying oneself with the church. Any young person who consistently witnesses will consistently be given excuses.

There are several general principles to keep in mind as you speak to a friend about Christ and are given an excuse. Excuses often hide the real problem. Soul winning is much more than answering excuses. The same excuse cannot always be answered in the same way. Each excuse should be dealt with openly and honestly. In dealing with excuses, the Scripture should be used naturally and in the light of its best interpretation.[1]

Anyone who witnesses will find that excuses fall into a pattern. If you learn how to answer several basic excuses, you can handle yourself in most situations. Always be honest. If someone gives an excuse for which you have no answer, admit it. Make a date with the person to return. Do your homework to find the answer and keep your prearranged appointment. Master the following simple procedures for dealing with some heavy excuses.

"I Don't Understand Enough."

Pascal, the French philosopher and mathematician, pointed out

[1] Kenneth Chafin, "What to Do with Excuses."

that the supreme function of reason is to show man that some things are beyond reason. With all our knowledge there are some things that the most brilliant person cannot understand. God does not expect any person to understand all the mysteries of his kingdom. He does not expect anyone to comprehend all there is to know about the doctrines of incarnation, virgin birth, crucifixion, resurrection and second coming. God does not expect us to understand all there is to know about the doctrines of conversion, regeneration, sanctification. He does expect us to come to Jesus Christ and confess him as Savior.

In Mark 8:38 Jesus said, "Whosoever therefore shall be ashamed of me and of my words in this adulterous and sinful generation; of him also shall the Son of man be ashamed, when he cometh in the glory of his Father with the holy angels."

If one understands enough to realize that sin has separated him from God and that God sent Christ to bridge the sin gap, he understands enough to be saved.

"The Great Number of Denominations Is Confusing."

As long as people are people, there will be differences of opinion. As long as there are differences of opinion, there will be different church denominations. The Bible does not forbid different denominations. It does forbid rejection of Jesus Christ. God is not so concerned about what denomination one joins as he is about whether or not one joins himself to Jesus Christ.

John 3:36 says, "He that believeth on the Son hath everlasting life: and he that believeth not the Son shall not see life; but the wrath of God abideth on him."

Impress upon the excuse-maker that he is not to be concerned about the denomination, but is to be concerned about accepting Christ.

"There Are Too Many Hypocrites in the Church."

Admit at once that there are hypocrites in the church. Tactfully point out that there are also hypocrites in other areas of life.

Say to the excuse-maker: "Some bankers are hypocrites. Does that mean that when you get a job you will take the money from your paycheck and bury it in a tin can in the back yard instead of depositing it in the bank? No! You will do business with the bank as usual. That is exactly what you should do.

"Some in the medical profession are hypocrites. Does that mean that when you get sick you will refuse to go the doctor? Of course not.

"The fact that there are Christians who are hypocrites does not mean that you should refuse to come to Jesus Christ and accept him as your personal Savior."

The non-Christian offering this excuse should remember that Christians do not attend church because they are perfect. They come to church because they want to do better. Just imagine how bad a person might be if he did not have the steadying influence of the church.

Point out that one must be careful about judging. Matthew 7:1-2 says: "Judge not, that ye be not judged. For with what judgment ye judge, ye shall be judged: and with what measure ye mete, it shall be measured to you again."

Romans 2:1 specifically says: "Therefore thou art inexcusable, O man, whosoever thou art that judgest: for wherein thou judgest another, thou condemnest thyself; for thou that judgest doest the same things."

Romans 2:6 says, "Who (God) will render to every man according to his deeds." In short, we will not be judged for the sins of the hypocrites. We will be judged for our own sins.

"Christians Are Often Cliquish and Unfriendly."

The same thing can be said about non-Christians. Unfortunately, all of us are guilty of running with one group of people and neglecting others. Christians ought to be different but, remember, they are not perfect. The lost person shouldn't be as concerned about being accepted by Christians as by Christ himself. Jesus said, "Him that cometh to me I will in no wise cast out" (John 6:37).

"I'm a Pretty Good Person and God Will Probably Accept Me as I Am."

It depends on what one means by "good." Some people feel they are good because they have a low concept of sin. If wearing lipstick is a sin, then all one has to do to live above sin is to leave off the lipstick. If it is a sin to wear jewelry, then all one has to do to live above sin is to leave off the jewelry. Many think they are good because they have a low view of sin.

Say to the excuse-maker: "Are you as good as the person in Mark 10:17-31 who came to Christ? This young man had never committed adultery, killed anyone, or stolen anything. He was not a gossiper. He did not bear false witness. Are you as good as he? You may be as good as this person, and better than most other people. However, if you have not accepted Jesus Christ, you are not good enough to be accepted by God in the judgment day."

Titus 3:5 says: "Not by works of righteousness which we have done, but according to his mercy he saved us, by the washing of regeneration, and renewing of the Holy Ghost; Which he shed on us abundantly through Jesus Christ our Savior; That being justified by his grace, we should be made heirs according to the hope of eternal life."

Ephesians 2:8-10 says: "For by grace are ye saved through faith; and that not of yourselves: it is the gift of God: Not of works, lest any man should boast. For we are his workmanship, created in Christ Jesus unto good works, which God hath before ordained that we should walk in them."

It is not by works that a person is made acceptable to God. It is by faith in Jesus Christ. If one is a moral person, he is too good to be eternally separated from God. He should turn from his sins and come to him through Jesus Christ.

"I'm As Good as the Next Guy. I'll Take My Chances."

Leroy Eims has a beautiful answer for this excuse which is a variation of the one above. It is so good I had to share it with you.

> The problem with this guy is, he just doesn't understand the sin problem. My answer to him is, "Yes, you're as good as the next guy, but have you taken a close look at the next guy?"
>
> The Bible clearly indicates that the next guy has the same problem—and it's big. "For all have sinned, and come short of the glory of God" (Rom. 3:23) indicates that every human is guilty before God and is subject to judgment. There are no "little sins" in God's view.
>
> The Bible also describes sin as going astray. "All we like sheep have gone astray" (Isa. 53:6). We are like an archer trying to hit a bulls-eye and his arrows fall short of the mark. The person who compares his virtue with others is lining up one failure beside other failures and taking comfort in the company of losers! The only safe comparison is with Jesus Christ, "Who did no sin, neither was guile found in his mouth" (1 Pet. 2:22). This is the standard we must match—or beg God's forgiveness and cleansing! [2]

"I've Done Everything in the Book. God Couldn't Forgive Me."

Say: Thank God for your conviction concerning the power, penalty and effect of sin. You should have the same kind of conviction about

[2] Eims, *op. cit.*, p. 99.

the love and power of God to forgive your sin. Our sin can never exceed the grace of God.[3]

When the lost person confesses his sins, God is ready to forgive him. If God could forgive David of his adultery and murder; if he could forgive the woman at the well of her sins; if he could forgive Simon Peter of his denial of Jesus, he can forgive you when you come to Christ no matter what your past is.

"What Will My Friends Think?"

Peer acceptance is one of those things which most frequently governs the decisions of your friends. Many of them will be afraid of losing respect or friendship. One thing you can do is to show them that some of the most respected youth in school are Christians who will be excited about their Christian conversion.

An acquaintance of mine shared Christ with a college student. When he asked him if he would like to accept Christ he responded, "What would the guys in my fraternity house say if I took this step?" They listed the fellows who would object and ended up with six names. All of them were heavy drinkers and poor students. My friend asked, "Would you rather have your life controlled by six drunks or by God?" He chose Christ.[4]

Young people must realize that some day they will stand before God alone. What God thinks about them is far more important than what their friends think of them. Revelations 20:15 says: "And whosoever was not found written in the book of life was cast into the lake of fire."

"I Want to Have Fun."

This excuse is given by those who have erroneous ideas about God and the true nature of fun. In answering the excuse, you should

[3] *Ibid.*, p. 98.
[4] *Ibid.*, p. 101.

point out that God is not a celestial killjoy looking over the banisters of heaven who, when he sees someone on earth having a good time, says, "Cut that out down there." Rather God intended for his children to have a good time. He created humans with good-times drives and capacities.

Because he knew what was best for us he outlined some boundaries for our fun. He wants us to have all the sex we want—within marriage. Outside of marriage sex creates anxieties, hostilities, guilt complexes, and is not best for us. God wants us to have some highs in life. However, the high produced by drugs and alcohol are but cheap substitutes for real paradise. Ephesians 5:18 says, "And be not drunk with wine, wherein is excess; but be filled with the Spirit." The joy that Jesus gives doesn't end with a hangover. It doesn't have to be pumped up every three or four hours. This brings us to the basic nature of sin. Sin is nothing but the illicit fulfillment of all that God wants us to have in wholesome ways. If a person wants joy, real joy, wonderful joy, he should let Jesus come into his heart. Jesus gives a joy which no one can take away (John 16:22c).

"I'm Not Ready."

If the person honestly doesn't understand enough, give him time to learn the essential truths necessary to become a Christian. Try to establish a Bible study time together. Start slow. Cover the necessary Bible truths but come to the point where you call for a commitment.

If it is apparent that this excuse is a cop-out, show that saying no to Jesus is a dangerous thing. It is dangerous to say no because of the impending wrath of God that hangs over the lost. Job 36:18 says, "Because there is wrath, beware lest he take thee away with his stroke: then a great ransom cannot deliver thee."

There is a danger of the drifting and hardened heart. Each time a person says no to Christ, it becomes easier to say no the next time. At last, one's heart can become so hardened that Christ can knock with the sound of an atomic bomb and the hardened sinner cannot hear.

Hebrews 3:7-8 suggests, "The Holy Ghost saith, Today if ye will hear his voice, Harden not your hearts."

Delay in accepting Christ is dangerous because of accidents and death. How far away is death? Death is just one breath away, one heartbeat away, one malignant cell away, one car accident away.

Proverbs 27:1 says, "Boast not thyself of tomorrow; for thou knowest not what a day may bring forth." Since no one has a guarantee of tomorrow, one should accept Christ now.

Do what you can to help people make decisions for Christ. Remember that one never wins an argument! Do not argue! Deal tenderly with excuses and pray that the Holy Spirit will remove them and bring salvation.

"You may be the final link in a chain that connects a person to Christ—or you may be one of the essential earlier links that help complete the eventual union." [5]

---

[5] Eims, *op. cit.*, p. 105.

XIII

My Witnessing Commitment

When Jesus called Peter and Andrew to follow him, he said, "Come ye after me and I will make you to become fishers of men" (Mark 1:17). The words "make you to become" indicate that learning how to share Christ doesn't come with the snap of the fingers. To become an accomplished witness takes time, practice and a stick-to-it-iveness. Somewhere along the way, you must commit yourself to the task. Now is that time.

If you would commit yourself to becoming the witness God wants you to be, will you, here and now, sign your name to this suggested pledge?

MY WITNESSING COMMITMENT

I promise to make witnessing a part of my life-style. I will practice the necessary disciplines to sharpen my witnessing techniques. I will make myself available as an instrument through whom the Holy Spirit can speak. I furthermore promise to train new Christians to do the same.

Name_____

Date _____

If you would like to send to me an indication of the witnessing decision you made, I will be happy to correspond with you in the future to help you with problems that might arise. You can use the following form:

MY WITNESSING COMMITMENT

Dear Sir,

I have signed the Witness Commitment pledge. Please pray for me that I might fulfill my commitment.

Name _____

Date _____

Address _____
       City   State   Zip

Send to George E. Worrell
         306 Baptist Building
         Dallas, Texas 75201

Appendix for Youth Directors

The book *How to Take the Worry Out of Witnessing* can be taught at youth camps, retreats, and during Church Training. Every youth choir making a mission tour should be required to study this book. Ask your young people to get a copy of the book and study it until they know it from cover to cover. Your church could make no better investment than in purchasing one of these books for every young person.

There are many creative ways in which this book could be used to train youth in witnessing.

I. Retreats

II. Youth Camps

Often youth camps deteriorate into a preaching marathon. The Bible teacher and missionary preach to the young people. Add to that the evening preaching service and there is too much preaching and not enough participating. A time slot for witness training would offer variety and make a valuable contribution to youth who should be sharing Christ with their peers. Ask for two forty-five minute periods or one and a half hours for the witness training sessions. The creative activities will help you teach better and involve young people in participation. Tuesday, Wednesday, Thursday, and Friday morning would give six hours for this study.

III. Church Training

The Church Training hour could be used for witness training. One chapter could be taught for a quarter's curriculum.

IV. WOW Schools

The book could be used as curriculum material for WOW Schools. Contact the Home Mission Board, Youth Evangelism Associate, for information.

V. Creative Activities

One of the best ways to teach young people is to involve them in creative activities. Study the following suggestions. You may wish to conjure up your own creative activities.

Chapter 1—Is a Person Without Christ in Trouble?

Purpose of the Chapter: To help young people realize that their peers are *lost* without Christ and that God wants all people to have an abundant life on earth and an eternal life in heaven.

Materials Needed: Bible, scratch pad, blackboard.

Creative Activity:

1. Ask young people to form groups of four. Give them two minutes to share the benefits of the Christian life with each other. Give the entire group time to call out the blessings they have listed. Write the items listed on the blackboard.

2. Ask the young people to look in their Bibles for three minutes to find verses indicating the fate of the Christless youth on earth and after death. Romans 1:18 shows the corrupting process that comes to the lost. Revelations 20:15 and 21:8 show the destiny of the lost.

3. Discuss the three kinds of death listed in Chapter 1. Ask youth to call out the names of peers whom they fear to be lost. Make a permanent list for future visitation. The following form can be passed out to find young people.

Chapter 2—What Does My Personal Life Have to Do with It?

Purpose of the Chapter: To show that if young people are certain of their salvation, cleansed of their sins and uplifted by their daily time with God, they can be effective in their witnessing.

Materials Needed: Bibles, scratch pad, pencils.

Creative Activity: There are three main parts to this chapter including assurance, cleansing and a quiet time.

1. Ask young people to share their conversion experience with another person.

"Lost Friends" Card
(Size 4" x 6")

(Front)

Name_____ Telephone_____ Date _____

LOST FRIENDS
Please give the names and addresses (if known) of all
those you discover who are not Christians.

Name_____

Address _____

Lost person's name given by _____

Name_____

Address _____

Lost person's name given by _____

Name_____

Address _____

Lost person's name given by _____

-over-

Name_____

Address _____

Lost person's name given by _____

Name_____

Address _____

Lost person's name given by _____

Name_____

Address _____

Lost person's name given by _____

Name_____

Address _____

Lost person's name given by _____

Name_____

Address _____

Lost person's name given by _____

2. Divide them in groups of four. Ask them to describe their assurance in terms of a color. Give them one minute to think and two minutes to share. Some may choose green or gold to designate a healthy assurance. Yellow or gray may indicate caution or doubt. Black might describe the person who has no assurance at all.

3. Ask young people to turn to page 16 of Chapter 2 and underline the sentence, "You can't introduce someone you don't know anymore than you can come back from some place you haven't been." If you are to be an effective witness, you must know that you know Christ.

4. The second part of Chapter 2 deals with the fact that if we are to go clean we must come clean. Suggest that lost young people will put up with Christians who try to live the Christian life and sometimes fail. They will not respect a person who claims to be a Christian but doesn't try to live a moral life.

5. Give the young people five minutes to write on a piece of paper the sins which they feel hinder their witnessing. Ask them to fold the paper and write 1 John 1:9 across the page. Advise them to confess their sins daily and claim this verse for cleansing.

6. Use the illustration of the two wings of an airplane on page 18 to show that young people must live moral lives and share verbally the gospel if they are to be effective witnesses.

7. The last part of the chapter deals with the daily quiet time. Ask the young people to set a time in the morning for a quiet time and make a pledge to keep their date with God.

Chapter 3—God's Hidden Persuader
Purpose of the Chapter: To establish the fact that salvation is the work of God through his Holy Spirit.

Materials Needed: A large mimeographed blank star on white sheets of paper.

Creative Activity:
1. State that the reason the term "soul-winner" is seldom used

today is because human beings do not WIN souls. They share Christ. The Holy Spirit does the winning.

2. Pass out the mimeographed star. List the five-point work of the Holy Spirit. (See Chapter 3, page 22.)

3. Ask young people to write the different phases of the Holy Spirit's work of salvation in each point of the star.

4. Challenge them to thumbtack the star on the wall in their room. This will help them to keep the work of the Holy Spirit firmly before their eyes. It will also provide theological teaching for other members in the family.

Chapter 4—Where Do I Come In?

Purpose of the Chapter: To show the relationship between the Holy Spirit, the witness and the non-Christian. The Holy Spirit does the saving work but he needs human beings through whom to work.

Materials Needed: Chapter 4 of the book.

Creative Activity: The one thing that will take the worry out of witnessing as much as anything is to learn this motto: "Successful witnessing is sharing Christ in the power of the Holy Spirit and leaving the results to God."

1. Ask the young people to turn to page 29. Read the motto out loud. Then ask class members to read it out loud together three times.

2. Ask them to close their eyes and say it.

3. State that if they share Christ in the power of the Holy Spirit, they have successfully witnessed whether the person says yes or no.

4. Use the illustrations found in the chapter to illustrate this truth.

5. Refer the youth to the imperatives Be Available, Hang Loose, and Be Sensitive in Chapter 4.

6. Under the topic "Be Sensitive" show the group that experience including fumbled and touchdown efforts will help them to discern the leading of the Spirit in witnessing.

7. Use a personal experience to show that the more they witness

the more sensitive they will become to the Holy Spirit.

Chapter 5—The Power Keys

Purpose of the Chapter: To show how a person can be controlled by the Holy Spirit.

Materials Needed: Mimeographed test.

Creative Activity: Pass out the following test. It will help to reveal the depth of knowledge your youth have on the Spirit-filled life. Then discuss the chapter.

TEST

True—False

1. It is estimated that a large majority of Christians have never made the wonderful discovery of the Spirit-filled life. _____

2. The Spirit-filled life is reserved for saints only. _____

3. The command to be filled with the Spirit is found in Ephesians 4:30. _____

4. To be filled with the Holy Spirit means to be controlled by the Holy Spirit. _____

5. My moral life has nothing to do with the in-filling of the Holy Spirit. _____

6. Faith is a strong prerequisite to being filled with the Spirit. _____

7. It is as important to keep the commandment "be filled with the Spirit" as it is to keep the Ten Commandments in Exodus 20. _____

8. The success of verbal witnessing is dependent upon inner spiritual resources. _____

9. Being filled with the Spirit should be a daily experience. _____

Fill in the Blanks

1. Five steps which are helpful in being filled with the Spirit are:

a. Recognize that the _____ _____ lives within you

permanently because of the _____ _____.

b. Realize that it is _____ expressed will that you be filled (completely controlled) by his _____.

c. _____ with sin.

d. Abandon _____ to _____ and his will.

e. _____ by faith.

MATCH THE FOLLOWING

1. Natural Man _____   A. Galatians 2:20

2. Carnal Christian _____   B. 1 Corinthians 2:14

3. Spirit-Filled Christians _____   C. 1 John 1:9

4. Crucified with Christ _____   D. 1 Corinthians 3:1-4

5. Dealing with Sin _____   E. Ephesians 5:18

Chapter 6—Witnessing Is Not That Hard

Purpose of the Chapter: To help young people realize that witnessing is as simple as carrying on a relaxed conversation.

Materials Needed: Mimeographed question sheets.

Creative Activity:

1. Ask the young people to form groups of four.

2. Pass out the following creative activity sheets.

CREATIVE ACTIVITY SHEET

Witnessing is two-fold. We go to witness and we witness as we go.

1. A slow student in math needs help for her classes.

(a) What would your attitude be toward this person?

(b) What would you do to reach this person for Christ, if anything?

2. Mr. Obnoxious is way out in sin.

(a) What would your attitude be toward this person?

(b) What would you do to reach this person for Christ, if anything?

3. My boy friend is not a Christian.

  (a) What would your attitude be toward this person?

  (b) What would you do to reach this person for Christ, if anything?

4. Mary is a wallflower and needs friends.

  (a) What would your attitude be toward this person?

  (b) What would you do to reach this person for Christ, if anything?

3. Give two minutes for each person to read and answer their question. Allow one minute per person for each to share how they answered their question.

4. For five minutes call upon the young people to volunteer someone from their group to discuss each one of the questions.

5. Go heavy on helping people with problems and sharing Christ in the process.

6. Point out that during their creative activity, the young people listened three times as much as they talked. Listening is a most important facet of witnessing.

Chapter 7—The Best Thing You've Got Going For You

Purpose of the Chapter: To help young people write their testimony, memorize it, practice it and share it with the lost.

Materials Needed: Mimeographed testimony form which appears on pages 49-50 of Chapter 7.

Creative Activity:

1. Pass out testimony sheets and go over the rules for writing a good testimony. (See pages 49-50.)

2. Give young people eight minutes to write out their testimonies. Then ask them to share with a partner. Sharing the testimony is so important that young people should be given the opportunity over and over again.

3. Feature youth testimonies during worship services, joy explosions, and youth fellowships.

Chapter 8—How Do I Get Started?

Purpose of the Chapter: To teach young people how to break the ice and get into the witnessing conversation.

Materials Needed: None.

Creative Activity:

1. Ask two young people to work up Chapter 8 as a skit to demonstrate the methods of starting the witnessing conversation.

2. After they have finished go over the acrostic F-I-R-M.

3. Ask young people to practice the approach several times with a partner. Encourage youth to begin witnessing.

Chapter 9—A Witnessing Tool

Purpose of the Chapter: To teach youth how to use a witnessing booklet in sharing Christ.

Materials Needed: Five *Real Life* or *How to Have a Full and Meaningful Life* booklets for each youth.

Creative Activity:

1. Go over the chapter material. Then give participants the opportunity to introduce the booklet and read it to a partner. Time will not allow a full reading. Stop the young people after they have read about halfway through the booklet.

2. Instruct the second partner to begin reading where the first one stopped. The introduction is very important. Let them practice this over and over in this session and in those to come.

3. Make an assignment for the young people to read the pamphlet in a divine appointment.

Chapter 10—You Can Develop Your Own Plan

Purpose of the Chapter: To help young people develop their own plan of salvation without being dependent on a witnessing booklet.

Materials Needed: Scratch paper, Bible for each student.

Creative Activity:

1. Divide the young people into groups of four.

2. Give them twenty minutes to develop from the Bible their own plan of salvation.

3. Have groups report and begin to forge on the blackboard a plan that is suitable to all.

4. Have young people copy the final plan. Utilize the plan outlined in Chapter 10 for the final example.

5. Make an assignment for all young people to memorize the plan before the next session.

Chapter 11—What Do I Do When My Friend Says Yes?

Purpose of the Chapter: To give young people instructions for following up a new convert.

Materials Needed: Poster boards, marks-a-lot pens or crayons.

Creative Activity:

1. Ask young people to form groups of four.

2. Provide a piece of poster board and marks-a-lot pens for each group.

3. Ask the group to think of methods to encourage new converts to grow in Christ and write them on the poster board.

4. Tape the posters around the room and compile a master list on the blackboard.

5. Emphasize many times that growth takes time and Christians are responsible to win others to Christ and to help them grow up.

6. Talk about infanticide. To bear a child and cast it in a ditch to die is comparable to leading a person to Christ and then forsaking him.

Chapter 12—How to Deal With Hang-ups

Purpose of the Chapter: To familiarize young people with excuses they will normally meet in witnessing.

Materials Needed: None.

Creative Activity:

1. Ask ten sets of young people to take one excuse and demonstrate

it before the other young people. This will involve twenty youth and will help them learn as well as teach.

2. Form a Socrates club of young people who will serve as devils' advocates to constantly quiz the others about how they would handle certain excuses.

3. If the group is small, two or three sets of two young people, each man demonstrate the excuses.

Chapter 13—My Witnessing Commitment

Purpose of the Chapter: To encourage young people to commit themselves to a witness.

Materials Needed: Commitment form at the end of Chapter 13.

Creative Activity:

1. Have each young person turn to the thirteenth chapter. Ask him to sign the two witness commitment cards. Leave one in the book and send one to the author.

2. Indicate that they can expect correspondence from the author if they write about specific problems.